~ *The* ~
# Foley Fish
COOKBOOK

SINCE 1906
FOLEY

~ *The* ~
# Foley Fish
# COOKBOOK

Compiled by
Laura Foley Ramsden

Illustrations by
Lynn Sevigny

Book Design by
Connie Babian Grab,
GreenLight Graphics

Correspondence may be sent to:
Foley Fish
77 Wright Street
New Bedford, MA 02740

ISBN 0-9727901-0-1

Printed in the United States of America

The Foley Fish Cookbook is dedicated to

Frank Foley,

for instilling in us his legacy of quality,

and to the Foley Fish team of employees,

both past and present,

for making this legacy a reality.

Contents

A "Chef Fish" indicates a recipe provided by an outstanding chef, restaurant or specialty retailer.

Preface

FOLEY FISH IS A FUNNY LITTLE FAMILY BUSINESS that has been around for four generations. We sell seafood to restaurants and specialty retail stores across the country, much like other fish processors, but we are unique in a couple ways, which we believe to be the key to our longevity.

First and foremost, we don't strive to be bigger, we strive to be better. We search high and low for the very best source for each seafood item we offer. We find the oyster harvester who leaves his oysters in the bed for an extra year — moving them twice, just so the meat gets plumper. We travel to salmon farms across the Northeast to find the one farm with exacting husbandry and special, all natural feeds which produce a firmer, better tasting salmon. Unlike standard industry practice, our scallops are never soaked in sodium tripolyphosphate because this destroys the natural flavor and texture of the scallop. People think we're a bit crazy about our buying standards. We think this is the only way to secure the best tasting seafood for our customers.

We are, in the words of second generation owner, Frank Foley, "quality nuts". Once we source superior seafood, we work tirelessly to ensure every ounce of freshness and flavor is retained for our customers. Frank Foley was referred to as the Dr. Deming of the fish industry because of his unyielding commitment to quality control at each step of fish processing. This means a refrigerated fish plant, bacteria control systems and 100%, all natural processing. We even ship our fish in metal tins (at greater expense to the company) because the tins are vastly superior to plastic and Styrofoam in maintaining fish quality.

We care, a lot, about the state of the ocean and its incredible resources. We not only have generations of our own Foley family in the business, our employees in many cases represent multiple generations of Foley workers. We are surrounded by those who rely on the fishing industry for their family livelihood. Our buyers adhere strictly to all government regulations, quotas and size restrictions. We are one of the only fish processors with a representative on both the National Marine Fisheries Northeast Groundfish Advisory Panel as well as the Highly Migratory Species Panel.

We like to think we are different because we truly care ... about our fish, our customers, our employees, our oceans and our industry. It is the extra steps, the attention to detail and an unwillingness to cut corners that make our days perhaps a bit longer, but in the end, that much more fulfilling.

Foley Fish — The Family

THE FOLEY'S ARE A FISH FAMILY THAT LOVES TO EAT! Some families enjoy art, others music, others the great outdoors, the Foley's, however, are a food-focused family. We love to plan menus, prepare meals and most of all, we love to dine with family and friends. We're not "fancy foodies", but we do insist on the freshest ingredients of the highest quality. This has been true from the first through the fourth generation of Foley's in America.

Foley Fish founder Granddaddy Foley, or "M.F." as he was affectionately known, was famous for the fine food served in his Brookline, Massachusetts home. M.F.'s grandchildren share fond memories of opening the icebox at their grandfather's home to find heaping bowls of fresh cooked lobster meat. An invitation to Nanny Foley's Sunday dinner was prized. These meals were an event replete with fine china, crisp Irish linens and multiple courses of exceptional seafood.

M.F.'s son, Frank Foley, second generation owner of Foley Fish, continued the tradition of good eating at the Foley house. Fish on Friday was a must and Frank's wife Rita's baked haddock was a Friday night ritual. A nut for quality and freshness, Frank relished simple preparations, which let the fish shine. He believed that if you had the right raw ingredients, they didn't need to be masked with exotic spices or complex sauces. To this day, a fusion fan, Frank is not!

Today Mike and his wife Linda, third generation owners of Foley Fish, center their family entertaining, holiday celebrations and even nightly meals on great tasting seafood. Whether it is fresh shucked briny oysters on Christmas Eve, chilled Jonah crab claws with cocktails or grilled salmon with the season's first peas on the Fourth of July, our family continues to commune at the table with great tasting fish.

My husband Peter and I, as the fourth generation of Foleys, feel fortunate that many recipes have been passed from generation to generation and that the love and appreciation of food has only grown stronger. We offer this cookbook filled with new recipes and time honored favorites to share our love of great tasting seafood.

From our family to yours, Best Fishes!

— *Laura Foley Ramsden*

x

Foley Fish — The Cookbook

THE FOLEY FISH COOKBOOK grew from the Foley family and Foley employees' love of great seafood and our customers' and friends' requests for simple, delicious fish recipes. We realized that our archives and our customers were a wonderful resource for recipes so the compilation began.

The Foley Fish Cookbook consists of approximately 200 recipes that have been collected over the years. The late Stuart Gray, or "Chef Scotty" as he was affectionately known, a retired chef from the Coonamesett Inn on Cape Cod, taught all of us how to cook and left a legacy of great recipes. You will see many "Chef Scotty" originals within these pages — you can be sure these are time-honored favorites.

We also invited restaurant chefs and our specialty retailers from across the country who offer Foley Fish to submit recipes. Many responded, graciously providing us with wonderful recipes reflecting current tastes and trends in cooking. Many of these recipes feature delicious regional specialties.

Each of our recipes has been tested in the Foley Fish test kitchens. The Foley Fish team was subjected to hour after hour, day after day of fish tastings. We pan-seared, we deep-fried, we grilled, we baked, we broiled, we steamed, we souped and we stir-fried. We even converted some non-fish eaters during the process!

We recognize that your fish dinner will only be as good as the fish that goes into it. Therefore, we have also included information in our *Fish Basics* section that we hope you will find helpful in selecting and handling the seafood you purchase.

We hope you have great success with our recipes. We had a great time compiling them.

Fish Basics

IN THIS SECTION WE SHARE with you knowledge derived from nearly a century in the seafood industry. We hope to demystify fish so you can purchase it and prepare it with confidence. Our goal at Foley Fish is to provide "just caught flavor" with every ounce of seafood we ship. From buying to handling to shipping, we take extra steps to ensure we preserve every ounce of just caught flavor for our customers. We hope you will use our "secrets" to get the very best fish with "just caught flavor" for your family.

Beware the Fish Tales

"Just in today." "Fresh from the boat." How many times have you seen these catch phrases in seafood departments or advertisements? Unfortunately they mean very little. Even if the fish delivery arrived that day there is no guarantee that the fish is fresh. Even if the fishmonger headed to the pier and bought fish directly from the boat, that fish may not be fresh.

How can this be? Fish have a maximum shelflife (the time during which the fish is still good quality) of 14 days. The shelflife of a fish begins the minute the fish is caught. It will last 14 days only if the fish is iced immediately upon harvest and maintained at 32° thereafter.

Unfortunately, many boats are out for 7–10 days and do not travel with enough ice to properly store their harvest. This means that some fish "just off the boat" may already be spoiled by the time the boat returns to port.

Fish handling after harvesting also impacts freshness. Is the fish gutted immediately? Does the fish processor keep it iced through-

1

out the processing stages? Is the processing plant refrigerated? Are there any chemical additives? Is it shipped under refrigeration? These are all key questions in determining the freshness and quality of fish. If fish is not handled properly at each step, spoilage accelerates and flavor goes from "just caught" to fishy!

Pricing

Fish pricing varies greatly. Popular species often get a higher price than less well-known species. If comparing apples to apples, cod to cod, however, and a price at one store seems to good to be true, it probably is. Remember, when purchasing fish — you get what you pay for. Fish prices of identical species and even fish from the same boat can vary widely depending on the quality and age of the fish. The fish from the beginning of the trip may be 7–8 days old when landed and consequently will cost much less than the fish caught the last day of the trip. Some markets buy the 8-day-old fish because it is less expensive. They describe it as "just off the boat," which it is, but it is still 8-day-old fish. This fish will not improve with age and is not worth your hard-earned dollars at any price!

Buying with Confidence

If you follow the steps we recommend in the next sections, "Selecting Your Fishmonger" and "Selecting Your Fish", your eyes and nose will be your best assets in determining fish freshness. You will be able to buy with the confidence that you are getting fresh fish with "just caught flavor" for your family.

Where Can I Buy Foley Fish?

Foley Fish ships from Massachusetts to specialty retailers across the country. If you are interested in knowing whether your market carries Foley Fish, just ask! If you are interested in having Foley Fish at your local market, give our name and email address to your local fishmonger. It's worth a try!

Email Foley Fish at: nbsales@foleyfish.com

Selecting Your Fishmonger

People often ask us, "Where should I buy my fish?" Here are a few things to look for when visiting your seafood counter to ensure you get fish with "just caught" flavor.

1. LOOK FOR FISH TO BE DISPLAYED WITH PLENTY OF CLEAN ICE IN THE FISH CASE.

The secret to maintaining fresh fish — keep it cold! Is your seafood provider doing everything they can to keep the fish cold? There should be a good deal of ice in the case but the fish should not touch the ice directly. Remember, fish want to be at 32°F. (Fish freeze at 26°F).

2. STEER CLEAR OF FISH DEPARTMENTS WITH A FISHY SMELL.

Fresh fish doesn't smell fishy. If you smell fish from the minute you walk into the department, there is old fish in the case and/or sanitation is not what it should be.

3. ARE THE FILLETS PILED HIGH?

If the fillets are away from the ice and piled high in the air, then they are being kept above 32° and spoiling at an accelerated rate. We have a saying at Foley's, "Pile it high, see it die!"

4. HOW IS THE GENERAL SANITATION?

Make sure the fish counter area is clean. Fish should not be sitting in pools of liquid. Employees should wear gloves when handling fish.

Selecting Your Fish

FOOLPROOF TESTS

The best tests to determine fish freshness are your own sensory evaluations. Foley buyers conduct Eye, Nose, Taste and Temperature tests before purchasing fish for Foley's customers. You probably won't head to the store with a thermometer but you can use Eye and Nose tests to get a good indication of the fish's freshness. If the fish pass these tests then you will be treating your family to the delicious, "just caught" flavor of truly fresh seafood. We recommend the following:

NOSE

Ask your fishmonger to allow you to sniff the fillets you are buying. Remember, FRESH FISH DOES NOT SMELL FISHY! If there is a fishy odor, you are smelling bacteria build up and you should not buy that fish. It will NOT improve with age, with washing off or with

3

lemon juice, and it will smell up your kitchen. *Note:* some seafoods will have a distinctive aroma — e.g. salmon has a cucumber-like aroma — but you should never buy fish that smell fishy, yeasty or worse, ammoniated.

EYE

There are many different types of fish, each with their own distinct characteristics. Following are a few visual guidelines for purchasing the most popular species.

WHITE-FLESHED FISH
Cod, Haddock, Flounder, Halibut, Ocean Catfish, Hake

The fillets of white-fleshed fish should be a natural, creamy shade of white with no yellowing, browning or dryness at the edges

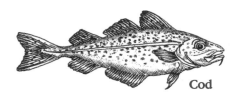
Cod

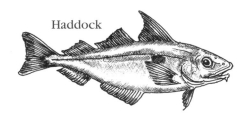
Haddock

Avoid fillets that look overly bright, shiny white or as if they have a film on them; this is evidence of chemical brining.

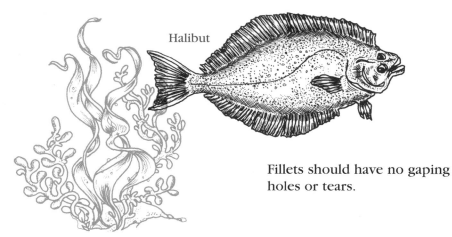
Halibut

Fillets should have no gaping holes or tears.

White-fleshed fish fillets, because of their mild flavor and shimmery appearance, are ideal for first time fish eaters and children.

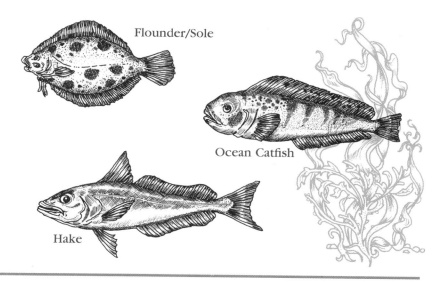

Flounder/Sole

Ocean Catfish

Hake

TUNA

Tuna should be red to burgundy red. Brown tuna is old tuna. Many times tuna steaks are wrapped in plastic to protect them from the air — this is a good practice.

Beware tuna that is a bright watermelon red color; this tuna has been "gassed" with CO_2. This process hides all signs of spoilage in the fish.

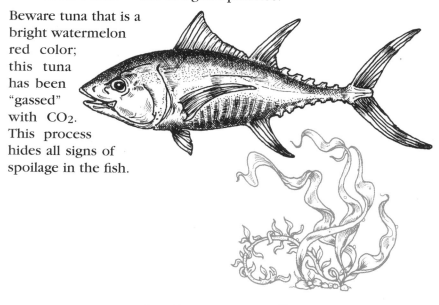

SWORDFISH

Look for a bright red bloodline and flesh that is translucent. Occasionally a "cherry" sword will appear. This pinkish-orange hue is normal—we believe it to be related to the fish's diet.

A brown bloodline or brown/grey flesh is a "no sale!"

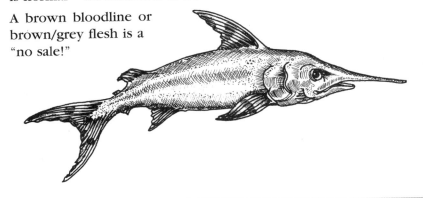

SCALLOPS

The natural color of scallops ranges from creamy to light tan to pale orange. A uniform white color is evidence of the industry-wide practice of soaking scallops in sodium tripolyphosphate to mask age and add water weight. Soaked scallops lack flavor, have a jelly-like consistency and will not brown effectively. Always ask for "all natural" scallops.

SHELLFISH

Mussels may gape slightly but should close when cupped in one's hand. Other shellfish such as hardshell clams and oysters should be closed when purchased. Discard any dead (open) shellfish before cooking.

6

DARK-MEATED FILLETS
Dark-meated fillets should look moist and not dried out or brown. Don't be afraid of dark-meated fillets such as Mahi Mahi, Pollock or Bluefish; they cook up light and flaky.

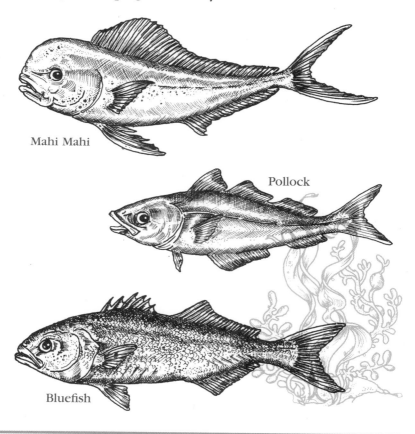

Mahi Mahi

Pollock

Bluefish

Storing Fish at Home

It is always best to prepare fish within 1–2 days of purchase because a home refrigerator is not cold enough to effectively preserve "just caught" flavor for longer than 48 hours. Here are a few tips for home storage.

IN THE REFRIGERATOR
Remember, keeping fish cold is the key to keeping it delicious. Take fish directly home from the store. Unwrap the packaging and place fish in a glass dish and cover. Store fish in the coldest portion of

your refrigerator — typically the back corner of the bottom shelf. Do not freeze fish that is past its prime; it will not improve in your home freezer.

IN THE FREEZER

Freeze fish the day you purchase it. Wrap it in plastic wrap and place into a zip-top plastic freezer bag, expelling all the air as you close the bag. If you have a large quantity of fish to freeze, separate it into several packages or it will freeze too slowly to maintain quality. If fish is frozen when purchased, store in your freezer immediately; do not allow to thaw. If product has thawed, cook the same day; do not refreeze! Keep frozen fish no longer than 1 month. Your home freezer is not cold enough to completely retard the bacteria growth which impairs flavor and causes spoilage.

Preparing Fish at Home

THE GOLDEN RULE

Preparing seafood is easy! Fish is best when cooked at high heat for a short amount of time. This seals in flavor without drying out fillets. One simple rule covers it all:

> **COOK FISH IN A PREHEATED 450° OVEN FOR 10 MINUTES PER INCH OF THICKNESS.**

Following this simple rule, a piece of fish one inch thick will cook in 10 minutes, a piece of fish $1/2$ inch thick will cook in 5 minutes and a $1\,1/2$-inch thick piece will cook in 12 minutes. Meatier fish such as swordfish may take slightly longer. When cooking fillets, turn tail portion under to get even thickness and ensure even cooking.

DON'T RINSE

Do not rinse fish before cooking. Rinsing washes away water soluble proteins that give fish its delicious flavor.

DONENESS

We believe the optimum cooking doneness for seafood is medium-rare. At this state of doneness, whitefish will flake easily yet retain its natural shimmer. Tuna will retain a pink core and the center of scallops will be just lukewarm to the touch. If you prefer fish cooked to medium doneness, just add a couple minutes to cooking time. Do not overcook.

COOKING METHODS

Sauté

It is critical when sautéing seafood to preheat the pan before adding oil or butter. Also, do not overcrowd the pan, as the fish will not brown properly. Almost any fish can be sautéed with delicious results. For scallops and flounder, it is the preferred cooking method.

Deep Fry

When deep frying, be sure oil is at the proper temperature before adding the fish — we keep a candy thermometer for testing the oil and find that 375°F works well for most fish. Deep frying locks in moisture and is a great preparation method for many fish and shellfish including oysters, squid, scallops, flounder, haddock and pollock.

Bake

The key to success in baking fish is to have your oven preheated. Remember the golden rule: cook fish at **450°F for 10 minutes per inch of thickness.** We like to add a tablespoon or two of water to the baking pan to humidify the oven. Most fish lend themselves to baking but because of the thinness of flounder/sole fillets, we recommend that they be rolled if they are to be baked.

Grill

Oil grill racks and preheat the grill before starting the fish. Follow the golden rule of baked fish — **10 minutes per inch of thickness.** Turn fish once halfway through cooking time. To enhance your presentation with criss-cross grill marks, start fish in one direction, then after 2 to 3 minutes, rotate the fish 90 degrees. The best grillfish are: swordfish, striped bass, tuna, salmon, monkfish, halibut and mahi mahi. Grilling is also a good option for any fillet when put in foil, and for scallops and shrimp on skewers.

Appetizers

Our favorite seafood appetizer is a just shucked, sea-salty clam or oyster on the half shell. To us, this is perfection, a true taste of the ocean!

Knowing raw shellfish isn't for everyone or every occasion, we offer the following appetizer recipes. Our experience is that a party always seems more special when seafood starters are offered — these are our favorites ... Enjoy!

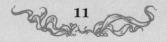

Appetizer Recipes

Grilled Tuna Satay with Wasabi Mayonnaise

SERVES 10

**2 tuna steaks (12 ounces each),
    cut into 40 – 1-inch cubes
2 cups mayonnaise
3 tablespoons soy sauce
1 tablespoon sugar
4 teaspoons fresh lemon juice
4 teaspoons wasabi paste or to taste
20 – 8-inch skewers**

In a bowl, stir together mayonnaise, soy sauce, sugar and lemon juice. Transfer 3/4 cup of this mixture to a small bowl and stir in wasabi paste. Chill, covered, at least 1 hour and up to 24 hours.

Stir tuna into remaining mixture. Marinate tuna, covered and chilled for at least 1 hour. Prepare grill.

Thread 2 tuna cubes onto each skewer and grill on an oiled rack set 5-6 inches over glowing coals until just cooked through, 2–3 minutes on each side.

Serve Tuna Satays with chilled Wasabi Mayonnaise.

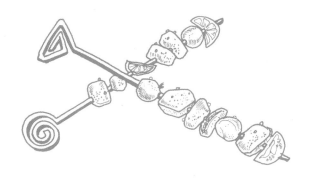

13

Zesty Hot Crab Dip

SERVES 30

1 pound Jonah crabmeat
1 teaspoon grated lemon rind
1 teaspoon horseradish
$1/2$ teaspoon garlic powder
1 ounce capers, drained
2 dashes Tabasco
2 cups mayonnaise
1 teaspoon Worcestershire
2 tablespoons chopped chives
$1/4$ cup fresh breadcrumbs or panko (Japanese breadcrumbs)

Preheat oven to 350°. Mix all ingredients except chives and breadcrumbs and pour into a buttered 2-quart casserole. Top with breadcrumbs and chopped chives.

Bake 20–30 minutes. Serve warm.

Hot Crab, Spinach & Artichoke Dip

SERVES 25

6 ounces Jonah crabmeat

$1^1/_2$ cups mayonnaise

2 14-ounce cans artichoke hearts, drained, chopped

$1/_2$ teaspoon salt

5 ounces frozen chopped spinach, thawed, well-drained

$1/_4$ teaspoon pepper

1 cup grated Parmesan cheese

$1/_4$ teaspoon garlic powder

$1/_2$ small onion, finely chopped

1 teaspoon fresh lemon juice

Preheat oven to 350°. Lightly grease a $1^1/_2$ quart casserole dish. Combine all ingredients into a large bowl and mix well. Transfer to casserole dish and bake until bubbly, approximately 35 minutes.

Serve hot with tortilla chips or crackers.

Spicy Grilled Shrimp

This is a Foley summer favorite — you can never make enough!

SERVES 10–12

**2 pounds large or jumbo shrimp,
    peeled and deveined
3 cloves garlic, minced
$1/2$ cup olive oil
$1/3$ cup puréed tomatoes
2 tablespoons red wine vinegar
2 tablespoons chopped fresh basil
$1/2$ teaspoon salt
$1/2$ teaspoon cayenne
skewers**

Combine garlic, oil, tomatoes, vinegar, basil, salt and cayenne. Add shrimp and marinate, covered in the refrigerator for 30 minutes.

Thread shrimp onto skewers. Preheat grill. Grill shrimp over medium-high heat, turning frequently and basting with marinade. Shrimp will take 6–8 minutes to cook through.

Classic Shrimp Cocktail

SERVES 20–30

**3 pounds 26/30 frozen shrimp
2 bay leaves
1 tablespoon salt**

Bring approximately 4 cups water to boil in large pasta pot. Add bay leaf and salt. When water is boiling, add frozen shrimp and cover. Cook for approximately 3–5 minutes until shrimp turns pink. Drain immediately and chill in refrigerator, covered.

Serve with Scotty's Special Cocktail Sauce *(see page 210)*.

Oysters Mignonette

SERVES 12

12 oysters
Mignonette Sauce
3 tablespoons coarsely ground pepper
3 tablespoons finely minced shallots
$2/3$ cup white wine vinegar

MIGNONETTE SAUCE: Combine pepper, shallots and white wine vinegar in a non-reactive bowl. Cover with plastic wrap and store at room temperature overnight. *Note:* Mignonette Sauce will keep for several months in the refrigerator.

TO SERVE: Open oysters and place on a bed of crushed ice. Top each with 1 tablespoon Mignonette Sauce.

Fried Oysters

SERVES 8

1 cup dry pancake mix
1 pint shucked oysters, drained
oil for frying
cocktail or tartar sauce (see page 210)

Put pancake mix into a large bowl. Add oysters and toss lightly until well coated. Shake off excess breading. In a large fry pan, heat 1–2 inches of oil until very hot. Place oysters, a few at a time, in oil to fry. Keep turning oysters until they are browned. Remove to paper towels. Serve hot.

17

Oysters Rockefeller

SERVES 12

24 oysters, opened
3 tablespoons butter
$1/2$ pound frozen finely chopped spinach, thawed
$1/2$ small onion, grated
1 tablespoon Pernod
pinch of nutmeg
salt & pepper, to taste
5 tablespoons dry white breadcrumbs
$1/3$ cup grated Parmesan cheese
3 strips bacon, cut into 1-inch pieces (optional)
$1^1/2$ cups rock salt

Preheat oven to 450°. Melt butter in saucepan over low heat. Add chopped spinach, grated onion, Pernod, nutmeg and salt and pepper to taste. Heat through then remove from heat. Place a generous amount on each opened oyster. Sprinkle with Parmesan cheese. If desired, place bacon strip on top.

Place oysters on bed of rock salt and bake for approximately 8 minutes or until bacon edges curl. Serve on rock salt to keep hot and to prevent juices from spilling.

For best results with oysters, store them in a bowl in the refrigerator with a damp towel over them but never let oysters sit in water. Oyster shells may be scrubbed prior to serving. If oysters are difficult to open, try putting them in the freezer for 2 minutes before opening.

Glazed Oysters

SERVES 12

36 oysters, opened
2 tablespoons butter, melted
$1/2$ cup fresh breadcrumbs
4 slices bacon, cut into 1-inch strips, partially cooked

Sauce

2 cups mayonnaise
4 tablespoons chili sauce
dash of paprika
dash of cayenne pepper
1 tablespoon Dijon mustard
$1/2$ teaspoon salt
2 teaspoons lemon juice

Combine melted butter with breadcrumbs.

SAUCE: Mix sauce ingredients together and refrigerate for 24 hours.

Preheat oven to 450°. Cover a baking sheet with rock salt. Nestle opened oysters into rock salt. Coat oysters with 1 tablespoon of sauce; sprinkle with breadcrumbs; top with bacon.

Bake for 4 minutes. Increase heat to broil and broil oysters for 3 minutes, just until oysters are heated through.

Scotty's Clamcakes

SERVES 10–12, 3 DOZEN CLAMCAKES

> 1 cup chopped clams
> 2 eggs
> $1/2$ cup clam juice
> $1/2$ cup milk
> 2 cups buttermilk pancake baking mix
> $1/2$ teaspoon dried tarragon
> vegetable oil for frying

Beat together all ingredients except clams and oil. Fold in chopped clams.

Preheat vegetable oil in deep fryer to 375°. Drop batter by rounded tablespoon into hot oil. Don't overcrowd. Cook in deep fryer until golden brown. Drain on paper towels.

Steamed Soft-Shell Clams à la Scotty

SERVES 4

> 6 pounds soft-shell clams
> 1 celery stalk, un-cut
> 1 small onion, cut in half
> salt
> $1/2$ cup melted butter

Put celery stalk, $1/4$ inch of water, dash of salt and onion in the bottom of a saucepan with a tight fitting lid. Place clams on top of celery stalk and onion and cover pan tightly. Turn burner to high and when liquid comes to a boil, steam boil for 10–12 minutes. Turn off burner. Let sit for 1 minute with the lid on. Drain and strain broth.

Serve clams with bowls of melted butter and broth for dipping. Remove skin from the "neck" of the clam before eating to get a terrific edible "handle" for dipping clams into broth and butter.

20

Foley's Clams Casino

SERVES 6

12 cherrystone or 18 littleneck clams
1 green bell pepper, finely chopped
1 red bell pepper, finely chopped
1 large onion, finely chopped
4 slices of bacon, cut into thirds
2 tablespoons grated Parmesan cheese
rock salt

Preheat oven to 450°. Open clams, saving the juice. Cover an oven pan with $1/4$ inch of rock salt. Nestle clams into salt.

Blanch peppers and onions together. Top clams with peppers, onions and a dash of Parmesan cheese. Cover pepper/onion mixture with 1 bacon piece and put in oven.

Switch oven to broil and cook until bacon is light brown and edges curl.

21

Foley's Cherrystones au Gratin

SERVES 6

12 cherrystone or 18 littleneck clams
rock salt
1 tablespoon breadcrumbs
Garlic Butter
1 stick unsalted butter
2 teaspoons parsley, chopped
2 shallots, finely chopped
1 pinch cayenne pepper
2 garlic cloves, finely chopped
juice of $1/2$ lemon

GARLIC BUTTER: Soften butter with a fork and mix all ingredients together. Form into a roll 1 inch in diameter and wrap in wax paper. May be refrigerated or frozen for later use.

Preheat oven to 450°.

CHERRYSTONES: Open cherrystones, saving as much juice as possible. Leave clams in the half shell but detach the meat from the shell itself. Nestle clamshells in an oven pan covered with $1/4$ inch of rock salt. Sprinkle each clam with breadcrumbs and top with a thin slice of garlic butter. Place pan in oven.

Switch oven to broil and cook for approximately 5 minutes or until breadcrumbs are golden brown.

Squid Antipasto

SERVES 2

$1^1/_2$ pounds cleaned squid, sliced into rings
1 teaspoon salt
$^1/_2$ teaspoon pepper
2 sprigs parsley
2 fresh tomatoes, chopped
$^1/_2$ cup olive oil
juice of $^1/_2$ lemon
mixed field greens

Place squid in a soup pan. Add salt, pepper, parsley, tomatoes and olive oil. Cover pan with aluminum foil to seal tightly and place lid over the foil. Cook on a very low flame for 2 hours. Do not remove cover during cooking. Keep flame as low as possible.

Sprinkle squid lightly with lemon juice. Serve at room temperature over a bed of mixed field greens.

Pecan-Encrusted Calamari

SERVES 4

1 pound calamari, thinly sliced into rings
salt
2 cups pecans
vegetable oil for frying
1 cup flour

Preheat oven to 475°. Lay pecans on baking sheet in a single layer. Roast 5–6 minutes watching closely to avoid burning. Remove from oven and allow to cool.

In a food processor, finely grind 1 cup of pecans, reserving other cup for garnish. Combine with flour; season. Toss calamari in pecan/flour mixture and coat well. Fry in hot oil for 1–2 minutes. Chop remaining pecans and use to garnish calamari. Serve immediately.

Crab Quesadillas with Cilantro Salsa

SERVES 10

7 ounces Jonah crabmeat

2 teaspoons mayonnaise

$1^1/_2$ cups shredded Monterey jack cheese

2 ounces mild goat cheese, crumbled

$1/_4$ cup canned diced mild green chilies, drained.

2 tablespoons chopped fresh cilantro

10 – 8-inch flour tortillas

1 egg white, slightly beaten

vegetable oil for frying

Cilantro Salsa

$1/_2$ cup fresh cilantro

1 cup sour cream

1 tablespoon lime juice

$1/_4$ teaspoon Tabasco sauce

Squeeze excess liquid from crab. Place in bowl. Stir in mayonnaise, Monterey jack cheese, goat cheese, chilies and cilantro.

Arrange 5 tortillas on counter. Spread crab filling over each tortilla, leaving a border of about $1/_2$ inch. Brush border with egg white. Place another tortilla on top of the filling and press edges together gently but firmly.

CILANTRO SALSA: Combine cilantro with sour cream, lime juice and Tabasco.

QUESADILLAS: Heat about 1 inch oil in large, non-stick skillet. Cook quesadillas one at a time for about 3 minutes each side, until browned. *Note:* For lighter preparation, bake quesadillas in a preheated 400° oven for 15 minutes, or cook in a non-stick pan lightly brushed with clarified butter or olive oil.

TO SERVE: Cut each quesadilla into 6 wedges and serve with Cilantro Salsa. These can be made ahead and reheated in a 400° oven.

Crab & Spinach Stuffed Scallops

A sit-down appetizer or first course for a special evening.

SERVES 8–10

1 pound jumbo sea scallops (16–20 scallops)
3 ounces Jonah crabmeat
5 ounces frozen chopped spinach, thawed, well-drained
$1/4$ cup heavy cream
$1/2$ teaspoon tarragon
salt & pepper to taste
dash of nutmeg
$1/2$ cup dry white wine
3 tablespoons butter, melted

Lemon Cream Sauce
$1 1/2$ cups heavy cream
$1/4$ cup white wine
3 tablespoons lemon juice
salt & pepper
roux (2 tablespoons butter, 2 tablespoons flour)
scallop cooking liquid

Preheat oven to 450°. Scoop out center of scallops using a melon baller. Mix crab, spinach, cream, tarragon, salt and pepper and dash of nutmeg. Stuff scallop with mixture. Combine melted butter with wine and pour into baking pan. Add scallops. Bake for 10–12 minutes. When cooked, drain cooking liquid and reserve. Place scallops on warm platter. Serve with lemon cream sauce.

LEMON CREAM SAUCE: Heat all ingredients except the roux over low heat. To make roux, heat pan over medium-high heat, add butter, then whisk in flour stirring constantly until golden but not brown. When sauce is hot, add roux until desired thickness. Adjust seasonings.

Dan Lombardo, Mendon House, Mendon, NY

25

Smoked Salmon & Goat Cheese Crostini

SERVES 10

8 ounces smoked salmon

Goat Cheese Crostini

**2 French baguettes, sliced diagonally into
$1/2$-inch slices**

olive oil

4 ounces goat cheese

Sauce

$1/2$ large red onion, chopped

2 tablespoons capers, drained and coarsely chopped

3 tablespoons fresh dill, chopped fine

$1/2$ cup honey mustard

$1/4$ cup Dijon mustard

CROSTINI: Preheat broiler. Brush each baguette slice with olive oil. Place on a baking sheet and lightly toast under broiler.

SAUCE: Combine red onion, capers, dill, honey mustard, Dijon mustard. Mix thoroughly.

TO ASSEMBLE: Spread goat cheese thinly on each baguette slice. Top with 1 teaspoon of mustard mixture and a small piece of smoked salmon. Garnish with dill sprig.

Smoked Salmon & Brie Strudel

SERVES 8

Mustard Sauce

$1/2$ cup sugar

1 tablespoon sesame oil

2 tablespoons soy sauce

$1/4$ cup rice wine vinegar

$1/4$ cup yellow mustard

$1 1/2$ teaspoons paprika

cayenne, to taste

$1/4$ cup chopped herbs (basil, parsley, tarragon, dill)

Strudel

4 sheets phyllo dough, thawed

1 stick sweet butter, melted

8-ounce brie wheel

Baguette

1 French baguette

olive oil

salt & pepper

Preheat oven to 400°.

MUSTARD SAUCE: Whisk together dry mustard, sugar, sesame oil, soy sauce, rice vinegar, yellow mustard, paprika, cayenne and chopped herbs. Set aside.

TO ASSEMBLE STRUDEL: Lay phyllo on table and lightly butter between sheets. Spread $1/4$ of the Mustard Sauce in a circle in the center of phyllo. Season brie and salmon with salt and pepper. Wrap brie wheel with sliced salmon. Place wrapped brie in center of phyllo and fold in opposite corners together to wrap brie in a nice package. Turn over so smooth side is facing up. Bake on greased baking sheet for 6–8 minutes. Let brie cool to room temperature.

BAGUETTES: Slice baguette and lightly coat with olive oil. Season with salt and pepper. Bake until golden brown.

TO SERVE: Place brie on platter and serve with toasted baguettes and Mustard Sauce.

Smoked Salmon with Mustard Dill Sauce

SERVES 10–15

1 pound smoked salmon, sliced

Mustard Dill Sauce

2 tablespoons red wine vinegar

2 tablespoons sugar

6 tablespoons olive oil

2 tablespoons chopped fresh dill, plus some for garnish

4 tablespoons Dijon mustard

1 tablespoon ground pepper

party pumpernickel squares

MUSTARD DILL SAUCE: Whisk together vinegar with sugar. Add olive oil slowly, blending well. Add chopped dill, sugar, mustard and pepper and stir until smooth.

Drizzle 1 teaspoon sauce on each party pumpernickel square. Top each with slice of smoked salmon. Drizzle 1 teaspoon more of sauce over the top and garnish with dill sprig.

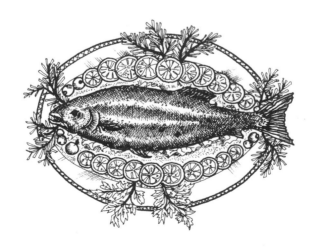

Citrus Cured Salmon

SERVES 24

1 side of fresh salmon (about 3 pounds),
   skin on, pin bones removed

$1/2$ orange; zest and juice

1 cup kosher salt

$1/2$ lime; zest and juice

1 cup granulated sugar

1 tablespoon coriander seed

$1/2$ lemon; zest and juice

1 tablespoon fennel seed

Crème Fraiche

1 cup heavy cream

2 tablespoons buttermilk

1 pinch kosher salt

Pat salmon dry and place on large sheet of plastic wrap skin side down. Combine all ingredients except salmon in a small stainless steel bowl (should resemble a coarse, moist paste). Generously spread mixture over the flesh of the salmon fillet until completely covered. Wrap tightly in plastic wrap and place between two sheet pans and weight down with several heavy cans or juice bottles. Place in refrigerator. Let cure for 18-24 hours.

Remove from refrigerator, unwrap and rinse in cold water to remove cure mixture. Pat dry with a towel and rewrap tightly in plastic wrap until ready to slice and serve. Serve with Crème Fraiche.

CRÈME FRAICHE: Stir cream and buttermilk together in a small stainless steel bowl. Add salt. Cover bowl tightly with plastic wrap and place in a warm corner of the kitchen, ideally around 80° or more, for around 24 hours. When culture forms, the mixture should be slightly thick. Gently whisk to combine thoroughly. Cover; refrigerate until serving.

Chef Michael Tuohy, Woodfire, Atlanta, GA

29

Dave Brite's Fish Cakes

MAKES 8 DOZEN

3 pounds haddock fillets

3 pounds cod fillets

1 tablespoon olive oil

$1^1/_2$ teaspoons fresh ground pepper

$1/_2$ teaspoon cayenne pepper

1 tablespoon paprika

$1/_8$ teaspoon thyme

4 bay leaves

2 tablespoons dry parsley

$1^1/_2$ teaspoons red pepper flakes or to taste

7 tablespoons Kosher salt

1 small bulb garlic, chopped

5 pounds potatoes, peeled, chopped

$1^1/_2$ pounds diced onions

8 eggs

1 cup chopped fresh parsley

Put oil and all of the spices (except fresh parsley) into a large pot of water. Bring water and spices to a boil. Add potatoes and half of the diced onions. When half cooked, add haddock and cod. Boil until fish is cooked through and potatoes are tender. Drain well. Roughly mash the potatoes and fish together.

Whisk eggs; add to fish/potato mixture. Add fresh parsley and rest of the onions. Mix well. Form mixture into 6-ounce patties.

Add oil to a frying pan until it is halfway up the sides; heat to 375°. Fry patties until golden brown on both sides. Allow patties to cool on plates lined with paper towels before serving.

Salads

31

Salad Recipes

Citrus Lobster Salad

SERVES 12

2 pounds cooked baby shrimp
1 pound cooked lobster meat
1 cup diced avocado
$1/2$ cup red onion, chopped
$1^1/2$ cups mayonnaise
zest and juice of $1^1/2$ oranges
zest and juice of $1^1/2$ lemons
zest and juice of 1 lime
$1^1/2$ teaspoons kosher salt
ground black pepper to taste
toasted brioche

Combine all ingredients except toasted brioche in a mixing bowl. Adjust seasoning with pepper, if needed. Serve on toasted brioche.

Chef Paul Weber, Foley Fish House,
Renaissance Hotel, Times Square, New York, NY

Mike Foley's Lobster Salad

SERVES 4

1 pound cooked lobster meat
1 cup coarsely chopped red grapes
$1/4$ cup slivered almonds, toasted
2 tablespoons curry powder
3 scallions, chopped
$1/2$ cup mayonnaise
2 tablespoons lemon juice

Combine all of the above. Serve atop red leaf lettuce.

Sea Scallops with Ginger-Beer Batter & Sesame Vinaigrette

SERVES 4

1 pound medium sea scallops (20–30 scallops)
flour for dusting
2 cups canola oil
1 pound baby field greens
toasted sesame seeds for garnish

Batter

1 cup all purpose flour
1 dash cayenne pepper
$1/2$ cup corn flour
$1/2$ teaspoon baking powder
1 teaspoon ground ginger
pinch of salt
12 ounces ginger beer or ginger ale
$1/2$ teaspoon salad oil

Vinaigrette

$1/2$ cup orange juice
1 tablespoon soy sauce
$1/4$ cup rice wine or cider vinegar
1 tablespoon brown sugar
pinch crushed arbol chili (or red pepper flakes)
1 clove garlic, chopped
1 teaspoon chopped chive or scallion
$1/3$ cup sesame oil

BATTER: Combine all dry ingredients. Whisk in ginger beer. Consistency should be like that of a heavy pancake batter. Stir in salad oil.

VINAIGRETTE: Mix first seven ingredients together then slowly whisk in sesame oil.

34

To PREPARE: Heat canola oil to 375°. Quickly dust scallops with flour then coat with batter and fry immediately until golden brown. Arrange scallops on baby field greens. Drizzle with sesame vinaigrette and sprinkle with toasted sesame seeds.

Chef David McGurn, Storrowton Tavern,
Storrowton, MA

Scallop Ceviche

SERVES 8

2 pounds Nantucket Cape scallops or
    small sea scallops
3/4 cup fresh lime juice
1/2 cup good quality olive oil
pinch of tarragon
pinch of thyme
1 1/2 teaspoons chopped fresh parsley
1 1/2 teaspoons chopped chives or scallions
2 shallots, chopped fine
1 1/2 teaspoons sugar
1 clove garlic, chopped fine
salt & pepper to taste

In a glass bowl, add lime juice slowly to oil, stirring constantly. Add remaining ingredients except scallops and whisk well. Gently fold scallops into mixture. Cover and refrigerate at least 24 hours. Serve chilled.

Note: The acidity of the lime juice "cooks" the scallops.

Tuna Caesar Salad

SERVES 4–6

1 pound tuna
salt to taste
1 tablespoon Cajun seasoning
$1/2$ tablespoon butter
$1/4$ cup vegetable oil
juice of 1 lemon
1 head romaine lettuce, washed; torn into
    bite-sized pieces

Dressing
1 large clove of garlic, chopped
juice of 1 lemon
1 egg yolk
1 pinch paprika
$1/2$ teaspoon Dijon mustard
$1/2$ cup olive oil

DRESSING: In a large bowl, mix together garlic, juice of 1 lemon, egg yolk, paprika and Dijon mustard. Add olive oil slowly, whisking until all ingredients are well blended.

TUNA: Cut tuna into $1/2$-inch cubes. Salt and season generously with Cajun seasonings. Place in refrigerator to marinate for at least half an hour. Heat butter and vegetable oil in sauté pan. Add tuna and sauté for 5 minutes. Remove tuna from pan, reserve pan juices. Return pan to stove. Add juice of one lemon to pan and bring to simmer. Pour mixture on top of the tuna.

TO SERVE: Just before serving, toss lettuce with dressing. Top with tuna and serve.

Scotty's Halibut Salad Vinaigrette

SERVES 6

1 pound cooked halibut, cooled; flaked
2 cups cooked diced potatoes
1 cup diced celery
$1/2$ cup diced onion
2 hard-boiled eggs, chopped

Dressing

2 tablespoons chopped shallots
2 tablespoons chopped, pickled beets
2 cloves garlic, chopped
2 tablespoons sweet relish
1 tablespoon fresh chopped parsley
1 cup red wine vinegar
salt, pepper and sugar to taste

Garnish

2 tomatoes, sliced
1 cucumber, peeled and sliced
2 lemons, sliced
1 head Romaine lettuce

HALIBUT: Preheat oven to 450°. Drizzle halibut with 1 teaspoon oil and season with salt & pepper. Bake for 10–15 minutes depending on thickness of fish. Allow fish to cool. Break fish into large chunks.

DRESSING: Mix all ingredients together. Gently fold in fish, potatoes, celery, onions and eggs. Refrigerate to blend flavors.

TO SERVE: Spoon onto a bed of fresh lettuce and garnish with tomatoes, cucumbers and lemon slices.

Cold Calamari Salad

SERVES 6–8

$2^1/_2$ pounds cleaned calamari
2 cups milk
kosher salt
juice of 1 lemon
2 tablespoons finely chopped cilantro
$1/_2$ cup finely chopped celery
$1/_2$ cup extra virgin olive oil
$1/_2$ cup finely chopped red onion
3 tablespoons rice wine vinegar
head of radicchio
lemon zest for garnish

CALAMARI: Soak calamari in milk, overnight. In a large pot, bring water to rolling boil. Add salt and lemon juice. Blanch tubes and tentacles no more than 3 minutes. Cut tubes into $1/_8$-inch rings and cut tentacles in half.

DRESSING: In a large bowl, combine cilantro, celery, olive oil, onion, rice wine vinegar and salt to taste. Cover and refrigerate for at least 2 hours to marry flavors.

TO SERVE: Toss squid with dressing and serve cold on radicchio with lemon zest for garnish.

Coconut Rice Salad with Mango & Shrimp

SERVES 4

1 pound cooked medium shrimp,
  peeled and deveined

Rice

$1^3/_4$ cups water

$3/_4$ cup light coconut milk

$1^1/_4$ cups uncooked long grain white rice

$1/_4$ teaspoon salt

Salad

2 cups cubed, peeled mango

1 cup diced seedless cucumber

$1/_4$ cup chopped fresh cilantro

$1/_4$ cup fresh lime juice

$1/_4$ cup thinly sliced scallions

3 tablespoons chopped fresh mint or 2 teaspoons
  dried mint

2 tablespoons minced, seeded jalapeño peppers

$1/_2$ teaspoon salt

RICE: Combine $1^3/_4$ cups water and coconut milk in a pan and bring to a boil. Add rice and $1/_4$ teaspoon salt. Cover, reduce heat and simmer for 20 minutes or until liquid is absorbed. Remove from heat and fluff with a fork. Spoon rice mixture into a large bowl and cool.

SALAD: Add shrimp, mango and remaining ingredients to rice mixture and toss well. Serve chilled.

Robert's Food Stores, North Madison, CT

39

Spinach Salad with Sea Scallops, Mango & Sugared Macadamia Nuts

SERVES 4

1 pound sea scallops (cut in half if large)
2 tablespoons sugar
3 tablespoons water
$1/4$ cup chopped macadamia nuts
cooking spray
2 tablespoons water
$1^1/_2$ cups peeled, chopped mango, divided
$1/4$ cup fresh lime juice
$1/2$ teaspoon grated fresh peeled ginger
$1/2$ teaspoon salt, divided
$1/2$ teaspoon poppy seeds
$1/8$ teaspoon black pepper
1 tablespoon vegetable oil
8 cups fresh spinach, stemmed & washed
1 cup vertically cut red onion

SUGARED NUTS: Preheat oven to 350°. Combine sugar and 1 tablespoon water in a medium saucepan. Bring to a boil. Remove from heat and stir in nuts. Spread nut mixture onto a greased baking sheet. Bake for 10 minutes. Spread evenly onto foil coated with cooking spray.

DRESSING: Combine 2 tablespoons water, $1/2$ cup mango, lime juice, ginger and $1/4$ teaspoon salt in a blender or food processor. Blend until smooth. Stir in poppy seeds and set aside.

SCALLOPS: Season scallops with $1/4$ teaspoon salt and pepper. Heat oil in a medium non-stick skillet over medium-high heat. Add scallops and sauté for 2 minutes on each side. Remove from pan, set aside.

To Serve: Arrange 2 cups of fresh spinach on each of 4 plates. Top each with scallops, mango and red onion. Drizzle with dressing and sprinkle with macadamia nuts.

Robert's Food Store, North Madison, CT

Baby Shrimp Salad with Mango

SERVES 4–6

1 pound cooked baby shrimp
2 cups of fresh mixed greens
2 mangos, cored and sliced into wedges
1 small red onion, sliced very thin
$1/4$ cup cashews, crushed
salt & pepper to taste

Vinaigrette

3 large shallots, minced
2 teaspoons minced roasted red pepper
$1/2$ teaspoon Dijon mustard
$1/2$ cup raspberry vinegar
1 cup olive oil

VINAIGRETTE: Combine all ingredients.

SHRIMP: Marinate shrimp in $1/4$ of the raspberry vinaigrette in the refrigerator for 1 hour.

To Serve: Toss salad ingredients with remaining vinaigrette. Place mango wedges on bottom of the plate. Top mango with salad greens. Add marinated shrimp and dust with crushed cashews.

41

Sea Scallops with Arugula, Lemon, Sweet Peppers & Avocado-Bacon Cream

SERVES 6, AS APPETIZER PORTIONS

12 jumbo sea scallops

Avocado-Bacon Cream

$1/2$ **pound apple-smoked bacon, diced**
2 just-ripe avocados, peeled and pitted
2 cups heavy cream
lemon juice, to taste
kosher or sea salt
ground pepper
cayenne pepper, optional
$1/2$ **pound fresh arugula**
1 green bell pepper
1 yellow bell pepper
1 red bell pepper
2 tablespoons finely chopped fresh parsley
zest of one orange, lemon and lime
2 cloves garlic, minced
coarse sea salt
1 tablespoon ground black pepper
2 tablespoons mild olive oil
3 lemons, peeled and segmented
$1/2$ **cup pine nuts, toasted to golden brown**

AVOCADO-BACON CREAM: In a sauté pan, render the diced bacon over medium-high heat until dark brown. Let bacon cool in its fat to room temperature. In a food processor, purée avocado with splash of lemon juice and pinch of salt until very smooth, like the texture of mayonnaise. Place purée in a mixing bowl, add cream and gently whip into avocado purée until incorporated and slightly fluffy. Fold in bacon and rendered fat. Season to taste with lemon, salt and pepper. Add a pinch of cayenne pepper if spiciness is desired.

SALAD: De-stem arugula and wash by submerging in cold water. Let arugula dry by draining for an hour. On a very hot grill or in a very hot oven roast the peppers, turning and blistering the skin on all sides. Place peppers in a bowl and cover for 15 minutes. While warm, peel and seed the peppers. Do not run peppers under water to peel and seed, as you will lose vital flavor. Cut peppers into $1/4$-inch strips.

SCALLOPS: Combine parsley, citrus zest, garlic and pepper in a bowl. Mix together with olive oil. Remove side muscle from each scallop. Toss fully in marinade and let stand for two hours. When ready to serve, heat a large pan/skillet or grill until very hot. Cook scallops on each side until very brown, about 3 minutes on first side and 2 minutes on second side. Scallops should be medium-rare with a little translucency in the middle.

TO SERVE: Toss arugula with peppers and lemon segments. Season to taste with salt and pepper. Place salad on top edge of the plate, displaying peppers on top. Sprinkle with pine nuts. On the front edge of plate spoon two dollops of the avocado cream and place a scallop on each dollop. Serve immediately.

Chef Casey Riley, Inn at Castle Hill, Newport, RI

43

Spinach Salad with Haddock in a Saffron Dressing

SERVES 6–8

2 pounds haddock fillet
salt to taste
3 onions
$1/4$ cup + 3 tablespoons canola oil
2 saffron threads (approx. $1/4$ teaspoon)
zest of 1 lemon
juice of 1 lemon
1 bag (16 ounce) baby spinach leaves

ONIONS: Preheat oven to 475°. Cut onions in half. Sauté lightly in 1 tablespoon oil then bake until onion begins to caramelize, about 20 minutes.

HADDOCK: Reduce heat to 450°. Sprinkle fish with 1 tablespoon oil and salt to taste. Bake for 10–12 minutes, depending on thickness of fillet. Let cool.

SAFFRON DRESSING: Heat saucepan. Add enough canola oil (about 1 tablespoon) to coat bottom. Add saffron threads and watch closely. Cook until they smell toasted, adding oil if they cook too fast. Remove from heat. Mix with lemon zest, lemon juice. Whisk in $1/4$ cup oil to complete dressing.

TO SERVE: Wash and drain baby spinach, put in bowl and add roasted onion. Add fish. Toss all with dressing.

Chef Kerry Romainello, Westport Rivers Vineyard, Westport, MA

Shrimp, Corn & Red Pepper Salad

SERVES 4–6

$1^1/_2$ cups cooked baby shrimp
$1/_2$ cup frozen corn kernels, thawed, drained
1 cup diced red bell pepper
1 15-ounce can black beans, drained, rinsed
2 tablespoons chopped fresh cilantro
$1/_2$ cup chopped green onions
2 tablespoons fresh lime juice
1 tablespoon grated lime zest
$1/_2$ teaspoon hot pepper sauce
2 tablespoons mayonnaise
salt & pepper to taste

In a medium bowl, toss together corn, shrimp, red pepper, black beans, cilantro, green onion, lime juice, lime zest and hot pepper sauce. Mix in mayonnaise. Season with salt & pepper. Chill until serving.

This salad is best if made 1 day ahead.

There are great differences in the baby shrimp available in the marketplace. Beware cooked baby shrimp from the Far East as most have been heavily processed. Foley cooked baby shrimp is all natural "Pandalus Borealis" from New Brunswick, Canada.

Mussels Dressed to Dill

SERVES 4

1 pound mussels, rinsed & debearded
1 cup white wine
1 cup water
1 head bibb lettuce

Dill Dressing

1 tablespoon chopped fresh dill
$1/2$ cup mayonnaise
1 tablespoon chopped scallions
1 teaspoon Dijon mustard

MUSSELS: Place mussels in large saucepan with white wine and water. Cover and boil for 2 minutes or until mussels open. Shake pot so mussels cook evenly. Drain mussels and remove meats from shells. Allow to cool.

DRESSING: Combine ingredients and mix thoroughly.

TO SERVE: Fold mussels gently into dressing and serve on a bed of bibb lettuce.

Soups, Stews & Chowders

Soups, Stews & Chowders Recipes

Foley's Creamy Fish Chowder

SERVES 6–8

**1 pound pollock or ocean catfish fillets,
cut into 1-inch pieces**
$1/2$ pound butter
1 cup chopped onion
1 cup chopped raw potatoes
2–4 cups fish stock (or water or clam juice)
salt & pepper
2 bay leaves
2 cups light cream
2 cups milk

Melt butter in saucepan. Add chopped onions and potatoes. "Sweat" together for 5 minutes (cook without browning). Add enough fish stock to barely cover potatoes and onions. Cook slowly until both are soft but not mushy. Add fish on top of onions and potatoes. Cover tightly and let steam for approximately 10 minutes.

Season well with salt and pepper and 2 bay leaves.

Add light cream and milk. Reheat but *do not boil*. Remove bay leaves and serve very hot. If thicker chowder is preferred, add a small amount of cornstarch mixed with milk.

Serve hot with slices of crusty bread.

Scotty's New England Clam Chowder

SERVES 8–10

4 pounds chopped clams
3 sticks of butter
3 medium onions, chopped
1 teaspoon thyme
salt & pepper to taste
3 bay leaves
1 tablespoon fresh tarragon
6 medium potatoes, peeled and diced
4 leveled tablespoons of flour
1 pint light cream
1 pint heavy cream
1 pint milk

Melt butter at low temperature. Add onions. Sweat at low temperature and season with thyme, black pepper, salt, bay leaves and tarragon (only use if fresh is available).

Put potatoes in a separate pot, barely covering them with water. Cook over medium-high heat, stirring occasionally but do not full boil.

When onions are transparent, add 4 leveled tablespoons of flour and stir for 3 minutes to obtain a roux. Add chopped clams, juice and all, and stir constantly while bringing to a boil.

Add potatoes with 1 cup of their cooking water. Stir constantly over low heat until mixture thickens; do not allow to simmer or soup will curdle. Add light and heavy cream and bring the chowder to just below a simmer. Slowly add enough milk to reach desired consistency; heat through. Taste; adjust seasonings. Warm the cups before serving.

Scotty's Manhattan Clam Chowder

SERVES 6–8

1 quart chopped clams & their juice
3 tomatoes, peeled and diced or 1 can chopped
$1/2$ cup butter
$1/4$ teaspoon crushed red pepper or to taste
1 clove garlic, crushed
1 cup diced onion
1 cup diced green pepper
1 cup diced sweet red pepper
pinch of thyme
pinch of basil
2 cups tomato juice
chopped parsley for garnish

Sauté vegetables with garlic and herbs in butter for 5 minutes. Add clam juice and tomato juice. Cook until vegetables are just cooked. Add chopped clams and heat through. Garnish with chopped parsley.

Chopped clams are best fresh from your seafood case (rather than canned or frozen). Chopped clams are the gigantic New England sea clams which have been harvested from the North Atlantic by offshore commercial clam boats. The clams are then shucked, chopped and packed in gallons. It is important to find all-natural clams with no sodium tripolyphosphate or MSG.

Risotto with Mussels

SERVES 6–8

5 pounds mussels, debearded & rinsed
$1^1/_2$ cups dry white wine
1 cup fresh Italian parsley
2 garlic cloves
5 cups clam juice or fish broth
$1/_2$ cup olive oil
4 shallots (or 1 medium onion) finely chopped
1 pinch dried red chili pepper flakes
2 cups arborio rice
salt & pepper to taste

MUSSELS: Place cleaned mussels with the wine in a sauté pan and cover. Boil for 3–4 minutes until all mussels open (discard the closed ones). Remove mussels from pan, reserving liquid. Save a dozen of the nicest mussels for garnish. Remove meats from remaining shells and chop. Strain liquid through a strainer lined with cheesecloth. Reserve.

RISOTTO: Chop together parsley and garlic. Combine chopped mussel meats with half of parsley/garlic mix and set aside. In a saucepan, heat clam juice to a gentle simmer. Continue to simmer while cooking the rice. Heat olive oil in a heavy-bottomed saucepan. Add chopped shallots. Sauté until translucent. Add remaining parsley/garlic mix with a pinch of chili pepper and cook for 1 more minute. Add rice and stir to coat with oil. Cook until translucent, 2–3 minutes. Add strained mussel liquid and stir in until absorbed. Add the simmering clam juice one ladle at a time, stirring constantly until liquid is absorbed. When rice is cooked to al dente, stir in chopped mussels.

TO SERVE: Taste and adjust seasonings as desired. Serve in dishes garnished with whole mussels and parsley leaves.

Mussel Jambalaya

SERVES 6

2 pounds mussels, steamed & removed from shells
1 cup dry white wine
2 tablespoons cooking oil
2 tablespoons butter
1 cup onion, finely chopped
3 cloves garlic, finely chopped
2 cups long grain rice
2 ribs celery, chopped
1 green pepper, chopped
1 cup diced, smoked ham
$1/4$ teaspoon nutmeg
$1/4$ teaspoon ground cloves
4 cups hot chicken broth
2 cups canned Italian plum tomatoes, well drained
freshly ground pepper and Tabasco to taste
parsley

MUSSELS: Rinse mussels under running water to remove sand. Remove beards (byssal threads) from mussels and place debearded mussels in large saucepan. Add wine, cover and bring to a full boil. Boil for 2–3 minutes until mussels are open. Shake pot so mussels cook evenly. Discard any mussels that don't open.

JAMBALAYA: In a Dutch oven, sauté onions and garlic in butter and oil. Add raw rice. Cook, stirring until rice is golden. Stir in remaining ingredients except mussels. Bring to a boil, reduce heat and simmer, covered, 25 minutes or until rice has absorbed liquid.

Taste for seasoning and add more broth if desired. Carefully mix in steamed mussel meats and any of their cooking liquid. Sprinkle with parsley and serve.

Foley's Basic Fish Stock

YIELDS 6 CUPS

bones from 6 to 8 mild, non-oily fish
   (e.g.: cod, haddock, flounder)
$1^1/_2$ onions, chopped
12 mushroom stems, chopped
1 stalk celery
juice of $1/_2$ lemon
bunch of parsley
1 tablespoon salt
2 bay leaves
10 whole peppercorns
1 teaspoon fresh thyme
$1/_2$ gallon white wine
$1^1/_2$ gallons cold water

Wash blood from fish frames; remove and discard heads, tails, fins and excess innards. Break the bones. Place all ingredients in a large pot. Add wine and water and bring to a fast boil. Reduce heat. Cover and simmer for 30–40 minutes. Strain liquid through cheesecloth. Fish stock may be frozen.

Traditional Escalloped Oysters

SERVES 4

1 pint oysters
saltine crackers
butter
1 tablespoon light cream

Preheat oven to 400°. Crush saltines to make rough crumbs. Mix with enough melted butter to make a dry paste. Place half crumb mixture in a small casserole. Top with oysters. Add remaining crumbs. Sprinkle oyster juice liberally over top. Finish with one tablespoon of light cream. Bake for approximately 10 minutes until heated through.

Oyster Bisque

SERVES 4

1 quart oysters, drained with juice reserved
1 bay leaf
2 medium onions, chopped
2 stalks celery, chopped
$1/2$ cup butter
$1/4$ cup flour
$1/2$ teaspoon salt
$1/4$ teaspoon white pepper
1 pint light cream
$1/4$ cup sherry
fresh parsley, chopped

Chop oysters; set aside. Add enough water to oyster liquid to make 2 quarts. Add bay leaf, 1 chopped onion and 1 chopped celery stalk and simmer uncovered for 30 minutes. Remove from heat and let stand for 1 hour. Strain.

Melt butter in saucepan and add remaining onion and celery. Sauté until tender and transparent. Stir in flour but do not allow to brown. Remove from heat and add half oyster liquor stock, stirring constantly.

Return to heat and add remaining oyster liquor stock stirring until smooth. Add salt and pepper and cook gently over low heat 10 minutes. Add oysters and cream and simmer gently for 3 minutes. Stir in sherry just before serving in warm bowls. Garnish with chopped parsley.

Buehler's Buckeye Stew with Ocean Catfish

SERVES 4–6

1 pound ocean catfish fillets, cut into 2-inch chunks
$1/4$ cup olive oil
3 cups chopped onion
3–6 garlic cloves, finely chopped
1 cup chopped celery
1 green pepper, chopped
2 teaspoons dried oregano
salt & pepper to taste
red pepper flakes
1 small bay leaf
2 teaspoons fennel seeds
1 18–24-ounce can chopped tomatoes
2 cups dry white wine
2 cups clam juice
4 tablespoons chopped parsley
4 tablespoons chopped fresh basil

Heat oil in a large, heavy pan. Sauté onions, garlic, celery and green pepper in olive oil until tender (approximately 10 minutes). Add oregano, salt & pepper, red pepper flakes, bay leaf and fennel seeds and sauté for another 2 minutes. Add tomatoes and heat for 3 minutes. Add wine and clam juice and cook for 10 minutes. Add fish and cook for 5–8 minutes. Add parsley and chopped basil. Remove bay leaf and serve.

Buehler's Food Markets, Wooster, OH

56

Ocean Chowder

The entire Foley office raved about this chowder —
we think the secret to success is in the brandy!

SERVES 4

$1/2$ pound medium sea scallops (about 12 scallops)
1 pound cooked baby shrimp
6 ounces fresh Jonah crabmeat
olive oil
2 tablespoons minced shallots
1 tablespoon minced garlic
2 tablespoons brandy
$1 1/2$ cups clam juice
1 cup heavy cream
1 cup julienned (matchstick) potatoes
1 cup julienned carrots
$1/2$ cup julienned leeks
$1/4$ cup chopped parsley

BASE: Preheat a large non-stick sauté pan over medium-high heat. Add olive oil and pan sear scallops on one side. Turn and add shallots. Reduce heat to medium-low and cook for 2 minutes. Add garlic and cook for an additional 2 minutes. Increase heat to medium-high and deglaze with brandy. Add clam juice. Bring to a boil. Add shrimp and crabmeat. Reduce heat to medium. Finish with cream; season to taste. Keep warm.

VEGETABLES: In olive oil, sauté potatoes over medium-high heat for approximately 4 minutes. Add carrots; sauté until al dente. Add leeks and cook over low heat for 3 minutes; season.

TO SERVE: Place ocean chowder in a bowl. Mound the vegetables in the center. Garnish with chopped parsley.

Sweet Corn Chowder with Bacon & Sea Scallops

SERVES 4

$1/2$ pound sea scallops
10 slices bacon, (apple wood-smoked,
cut into 1-inch dice)
1 red onion, finely chopped
3 cups frozen corn kernels, thawed
3 cups whole milk
1 pound scrubbed red potatoes, parboiled,
cut into $1/2$-inch dice
$1/2$ cup heavy cream
2 tablespoons minced chives
hot red pepper sauce
salt and ground white pepper to taste

BACON: In a large pot over medium heat, fry bacon until almost crisp, 5 to 7 minutes. Use a slotted spoon to transfer bacon to a paper towel. Drain all but 2 tablespoons bacon fat, reserve drippings.

CHOWDER: Return pot to medium heat. Add onion and cook, stirring frequently, until soft but not brown, 5 to 10 minutes. In a blender or food processor, purée 1 cup of corn with 1 cup of milk; set aside. To the softened onions, add potatoes, corn/milk mixture, remaining corn and milk and cook, stirring, until potatoes are cooked through, about 15 minutes. *Do not let chowder simmer.* Add cream, chives, pepper sauce, salt and pepper to taste and cook, stirring occasionally, until slightly thickened, 3–5 minutes.

SCALLOPS: Heat skillet with remaining drippings over medium-high heat. Add scallops to skillet and cook, turning once, until cooked through, about 2 minutes per side. Transfer to a cutting board and cut into quarters.

TO SERVE: Ladle soup into individual bowls. Garnish with sea scallops and reserved bacon.

Untraditional Clam Chowder

SERVES 8–10

4 pounds chopped clams
2 sticks butter
3 medium onions, chopped
1 pound smoked sausage, diced
fresh thyme sprig
4 large potatoes, diced
1 16-ounce can creamed corn
1 16-ounce can cut green beans
1 quart whole milk
1 pint heavy cream

Melt butter. Add onions and smoked sausage and allow to "sweat". Add fresh thyme to taste. Boil cubed potatoes in a separate pot with just enough water to cover. Drain. Add potatoes to onions and sausage and continue to cook. Add corn and green beans. When mixture reaches a boil, stir in chopped clams and cook 2–3 minutes. Do not return to a boil. In separate pan, heat milk and cream until very hot. Add to pot and serve.

Chowder has become part of the Foley culture. We are constantly creating new chowders with whatever we find left in the kitchen after a customer visit or tasting session. Curdling the milk is a mortal sin but other than that, anything goes!

Lobster Chowder

SERVES 4–6

2 cups coarsely chopped lobster meat
lobster juice (saved during shelling process)
$1/4$ cup butter
1 cup sliced leeks
$1/2$ cup chopped celery
1 cup peeled and diced potatoes
1 cup chicken stock or water
2 tablespoons flour
1 cup light cream
2 tablespoons heavy cream
1 teaspoon minced tarragon
salt & pepper

Heat 2 tablespoons of butter in a large saucepan over medium heat. Add leeks and celery and sauté until just tender, 2–3 minutes. Add potatoes, lobster juice and chicken stock and simmer until potatoes are just tender, 10–12 minutes.

In a small bowl, combine remaining butter with flour and mash with a fork to make a smooth paste. Add this paste to the saucepan, followed by light cream, and stir to mix thoroughly. Simmer, stirring often, until chowder thickens, 3–4 minutes. Add lobster, heavy cream and tarragon; season to taste.

Seafood Stew with Lemon & Saffron

SERVES 8

1 pound monkfish, cod or ocean catfish
18 peeled, deveined shrimp
$1/2$ pound scallops
12 mussels in shells
12 small clams in shells
3 tablespoons olive oil
1 bay leaf
$1 1/2$ cups sliced carrots
2 cups sliced white onion
2 cups chopped celery
1 fennel bulb, sliced
3 jalapeño peppers
$1/4$ cup diced shallots
3 tablespoons roasted garlic
2 pinches saffron
2 tablespoons butter
2 tablespoons chopped fresh thyme
1 tablespoon dried mint
1 cup sherry
$1/2$ cup lemon juice
2 quarts seafood stock or clam juice
salt & pepper
$1/4$ cup parsley

Heat oil in large braising pan. Add bay leaf, vegetables, jalapeños, shallots, garlic (to roast garlic, brush whole bulb with oil and roast at 400° for 15 minutes or until soft), and saffron. Sauté until onions are translucent. Stir in butter, thyme, and mint. Add sherry and lemon juice to de-glaze the pan. Add seafood stock and bring to a boil. Poach monkfish, shrimp, and scallops in broth for 8 minutes. Add mussels and clams.

When shells open (6–8 minutes), add salt and pepper to taste. Garnish with parsley.

Authentic Louisiana Seafood Gumbo

*Don't let the long list of ingredients scare you.
This is delicious and not difficult!*

SERVES 6–8

$1/2$ pound crab meat

$1/2$ pound shrimp

$1/2$ pound oysters

4 tablespoons chopped garlic

4 celery stalks, diced

1 onion, diced

1 green pepper, diced

$2 1/2$ gallons Crab Stock (see below)

$1 1/2$ cups Dark Roux (see below)

$1/2$ cup diced tomato

2 tablespoons hot sauce

2 tablespoons Worcestershire sauce

salt & pepper

Crab Stock

2 pounds crab shells (or 1 pound crabmeat)

1 carrot

$1/2$ celery head

2 tablespoons garlic

3 gallons water

2 ounces tomato paste

Dark Roux

1 cup canola oil

1 cup flour

4 cups steamed white rice

$1/2$ cup chopped scallions

CRAB STOCK: Sauté the crab shells for 15 minutes. Combine the carrots, celery, and garlic into the crab. Keep searing for another 5 minutes. Pour in the water and the tomato paste. Simmer for about 40 minutes. Set aside for 15 minutes.

Pour the stock into a bouillon strainer. Set aside. (If using crabmeat, do not strain).

DARK ROUX: Heat oil. Whisk flour into oil. Cook at low heat until mixture is a dark chocolate color.

GUMBO: Sauté garlic, celery, onions and green peppers. Pour 2 gallons of crab stock and bring to a boil. Turn off the heat and pour the dark roux into the soup. Turn heat back to medium, simmer for 35 minutes. Add crab, shrimp and oysters to the gumbo. Adjust consistency, using remaining stock if necessary. Finish with diced tomato. Season to taste with hot sauce, Worcestershire and salt and pepper

TO SERVE: Pour the gumbo over steamed white rice in a soup bowl and top with chopped scallions.

Executive Chef Eric Branger,
Ritz-Carlton New Orleans, LA

Foley's Oyster Stew

SERVES 4–6

1 pint shucked oysters, with liquor
1/4 cup butter
4 drops Worcestershire sauce
salt & pepper to taste
1 pint heavy cream
1 pint light cream
fresh parsley or fresh thyme for garnish, chopped

Sauté oysters very lightly in melted butter. Add Worcestershire sauce, salt and pepper. Add cream and bring to just below the boiling point. Do not boil. Garnish with chopped fresh parsley or thyme.

Angeluna's Seafood Paella

SERVES 10

2 pounds smoked mussels

2 pounds cooked baby shrimp

2 pounds crawfish tails

5 tablespoons oil

5 cups carnaroli rice (or arborio rice)

5 tablespoons chopped garlic

1 large onion, diced

salt to taste

1 cup white wine

7 cups clam juice, warmed

2 cups sugar snap peas

1 cup green olives

1 cup diced tomatoes

1 pinch saffron

3 tablespoons fresh thyme

3 tablespoons fresh parsley

5 tablespoons Truffle Butter (see below)

Seasoned Salt

$1/2$ cup salt

$1/4$ cup marjoram

1 cup grated Asiago cheese

$1/4$ cup oregano

$1/4$ cup basil

2 tablespoons pepper flakes

2 tablespoons thyme

$1/4$ cup garlic powder

Truffle Butter

$1/4$ cup Seasoned Salt (see above)

1 pound butter

$1/4$ cup white truffle oil

64

Note: The Seasoned Salt and Truffle Butter make more than enough for one paella. Reserve for future use.

SEASONED SALT: Mix together ingredients and store in a dry place.

TRUFFLE BUTTER: Mix all ingredients and store, wrapped, in refrigerator.

PAELLA: Heat oil in large flat pan, add rice and stir until rice starts to color. Add garlic and onion, season lightly with salt. Add wine, cook down and add 5 cups clam juice in two parts. Reduce until dry. Add sugar snap peas and remaining 2 cups clam juice. Reduce until $3/4$ of the liquid has evaporated. Add olives, tomatoes, spices and Truffle Butter to heat. Stir in butter and check seasonings. Let rest 5 minutes then serve.

Note: The truffle butter adds extra steps and expense but it is well worth it!

Angeluna's, Fort Worth, TX

Finnan Haddie Chowder

3 QUARTS

$1^1/_2$ pounds finnan haddie
$1/_4$ pound salt pork, rind removed
2 small onions, peeled and sliced
4 medium potatoes, peeled and diced
salt and freshly ground pepper
1 bay leaf
4 cups milk
1 cup heavy cream

Blanch salt pork in boiling water for 5 minutes to render some of the fat; drain then dice. In a large saucepan, brown the rendered salt pork; then add onion and sauté until soft. Add potatoes and enough water to cover. Add salt, freshly ground pepper and bay leaf. Cover and simmer until potatoes are barely tender. Add milk, cream and fish; simmer 15–20 minutes. Remove bay leaf and serve.

Monahan's Fish Market, Ann Arbor, MI

66

Pasta

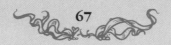

Pasta Recipes

Pasta with Sea Scallops in Yellow Pepper Sauce

SERVES 4–6

> 1 pound sea scallops
> $1/4$ cup olive oil
> 6 sweet yellow peppers, cored, seeded
>   and cut into $1/4$-inch dice
> 1 large yellow onion diced
> 2 garlic cloves, minced
> 2 tablespoons chopped fresh basil
>   or 1 teaspoon dried
> salt & pepper
> 2 tablespoons butter
> 2 tablespoons canola oil
> cooked pasta of your choice

SAUCE: Heat olive oil in a medium-size skillet over high heat. Add yellow peppers, onion and garlic and sauté for 10 minutes. Reduce heat to low, cover pan and simmer for 30 minutes. Transfer pepper mixture to a food processor. Add basil and salt and pepper to taste. Process until smooth. Remove to a saucepan and heat to boiling. Cook uncovered over medium-high heat, stirring frequently until reduced and slightly thickened, 5–10 minutes. While sauce is thickening, cook pasta.

SCALLOPS: Heat pan over high heat, add canola oil and butter. Sauté scallops for 3–4 minutes. Add yellow pepper sauce to pan and combine with scallops.

TO SERVE: Toss pasta with scallops and yellow pepper sauce and serve.

Sea Scallops in Red Pepper Sauce

SERVES 8

$2^{1}/_{2}$ pounds sea scallops
4 large red peppers
1 pint heavy cream
1 large shallot, minced
1 tablespoon olive oil
1 cup clam juice
1 tablespoon chopped fresh basil
salt & pepper to taste
2 tablespoons butter
2 tablespoons cognac
1 tablespoon anisette liqueur (such as Pernod)
1 teaspoon finely diced chives
1 pound green pasta, cooked

SAUCE: Roast red peppers, cool, peel and remove seeds. Purée in blender with heavy cream. In hot skillet, sauté shallots in olive oil. Add the purée of red peppers, clam juice, basil and salt and pepper to taste. Let cook until sauce becomes velvety and slightly thickened. Add butter. Remove from stove.

SCALLOPS: In another hot skillet, sauté the scallops approximately 2 minutes with a touch of butter. Add cognac and the anisette liqueur and flambé.

TO SERVE: Add the sauce to scallop pan and toss quickly. Sprinkle with fresh chives and serve immediately. Serve with green pasta.

Scallop, Clam & Pasta Toss

SERVES 4

1 pound chopped clams
1 pound bay scallops or small sea scallops
2 cloves garlic, crushed
1 cup olive oil
$1/4$ cup white wine
1 cup clam juice
pinch dried oregano
1 pound linguine
4 tablespoons parsley, chopped

Cook linguine in rapidly boiling salted water. Drain.

Sauté garlic in olive oil. When golden, add clams and scallops along with 1 cup clam juice and white wine. Cover and cook for 3-4 minutes until clams are heated through and scallops are cooked.

Uncover; add oregano and parsley. Cook for 1 minute to heat. Return drained linguine to large pot over medium-high heat. Stir in clam and scallop sauce. Toss with wooden spoon for 1 minute. Remove from heat and serve immediately.

Roche Brothers/Sudbury Farms, Boston, MA

Roast Loin of Monkfish with Penne Alfredo & Grilled Vegetables

SERVES 4

$1^1/_2$ pounds cleaned monkfish

4 cups penne

Grilled Vegetables

1 yellow summer squash, sliced into rounds

1 zucchini, sliced into rounds

1 ripe tomato, cored and cut in half

2 spears asparagus

Alfredo

2 cups heavy cream

2 sticks unsalted butter

$1/_2$ cup freshly grated Parmesan cheese, or to taste

$1/_2$ cup sherry

salt to taste

ALFREDO: Combine cream and butter in a saucepan and reduce until it starts to thicken. Add cheese and sherry. Reduce heat to simmer. Cook until sauce coats the back of a spoon. Season with salt and adjust the amount of Parmesan to taste.

VEGETABLES: Preheat grill. Once hot, brush vegetables with olive oil and season with salt and pepper. Grill vegetables until tender. Keep warm.

FISH: Preheat oven to 350°. Heat a sauté pan over a high flame until hot. Season monkfish with salt and pepper. Add vegetable oil or clarified butter to pan. Add monkfish. Sear on all sides. Remove to a roasting pan and finish cooking in the oven until medium-rare. Remove from oven and allow to rest.

TO SERVE: Cook pasta in boiling water and drain. Heat Alfredo Sauce in a large saucepan and add pasta. Place pasta in the center of a warm pasta bowl and arrange grilled vegetables. Top with roast monkfish.

Chef Jeff Evans, Steve & Rocky's, Novi, MI

72

Pasta with Smoked Salmon & Asparagus

SERVES 4

$3/4$ **pound smoked salmon**
$3/4$ **pound thin asparagus**
$3/4$ **cup butter**
$1^1/2$ **shallots, thinly sliced**
$1/2$ **cup white wine**
$1/4$ **cup lemon juice**
$3/4$ **pound flat pasta, e.g., fettuccine**
$1^1/2$ **teaspoons freshly ground pepper**
salt & pepper

Blanch asparagus, rinse with cold water and chop into $1/4$-inch pieces. Melt butter in sauté pan, add chopped shallots and sauté until soft. Add wine and lemon juice, stirring with a wooden spoon to deglaze the bottom of the pan. Cook until slightly thickened, about 10 minutes. Cook pasta. Combine salmon, asparagus and sauce with cooked pasta and pepper. Toss to mix. Add salt and pepper to taste.

Shrimp with Tomatoes

SERVES 4

$1^1/_2$ pounds rock shrimp
6–8 medium red ripe tomatoes
4 tablespoons olive oil
1 medium white onion, finely chopped
2 teaspoons salt
$1/_2$ cup white wine
2 teaspoons oregano
8 ounces clam juice
1 clove garlic, finely chopped
$1/_2$ cup finely chopped parsley
crushed red peppers, to taste

Scald tomatoes in hot water. Peel, seed and cut tomatoes into small pieces. Warm olive oil in large sauté pan. Add onion and let it sweat at low heat until onion is translucent. Add 1 teaspoon salt. Add white wine and let it evaporate. Add tomatoes and oregano and let cook at medium-high for 5 minutes. Add 1 teaspoon salt while cooking. Add clam juice and let it reduce by half at medium-high heat. Add rock shrimp and cook through. While juice is reducing, add garlic and parsley to pan. Add red peppers to taste.

Serve hot over a bed of rice or use as a pasta sauce.

Rock Shrimp are a unique species of shrimp with a very hard shell. They are harvested from Virginia through the Gulf of Mexico. Rock Shrimp have a firmer texture than most shrimp, more like lobster meat.

Baked Shrimp with Feta Cheese

SERVES 4

1 teaspoon olive oil
cooking spray
$3/4$ teaspoon dried oregano
$1/2$ teaspoon salt
$1/4$ teaspoon crushed red pepper
1 pound cooked, medium shrimp,
    peeled and deveined
3 garlic cloves, minced
$1/2$ cup dry white wine
3 cups diced (about $3/4$ pound) plum tomatoes
$3/4$ cup (about 3 ounces) crumbled feta cheese
4 cups hot cooked linguine, about 8 ounces
    uncooked
$1^1/4$ cup minced fresh parsley

Preheat oven to 350°. Heat oil in a large non-stick skillet over medium-high heat. Add oregano, salt, red pepper, cooked shrimp and garlic; sauté for 3 minutes. Spoon the shrimp mixture into an 11x7 inch baking dish coated with cooking spray.

Add wine to skillet; cook over low heat until reduced to $1/4$ cup, about 3 minutes. Stir in tomato and pour over the shrimp mixture. Sprinkle with cheese and bake for 10 minutes. Pour mixture over pasta and sprinkle with parsley.

Robert's Food Stores, North Madison, CT

75

Fusilli with Shrimp, Pan-Seared Ricotta Salata & Rapini

SERVES 4

1 pound 26/30 shrimp, thawed, peeled and deveined
1 pound fusilli pasta
2 tablespoons olive oil
$1/2$ pound ricotta salata, cubed
$1/4$ cup white wine
$1/4$ cup garlic, minced
4 ounces rapini, chopped
4 yellow tomatoes, quartered
3 red plum tomatoes, quartered
$1/4$ cup prepared pesto
$1/4$ cup pecorino Romano cheese, grated

In medium pot, bring 1 gallon of lightly salted water to a boil. Add fusilli and cook for 8–10 minutes. Drain pasta and set aside.

In a medium skillet, heat olive oil. Add ricotta and brown on all sides. Remove ricotta from pan, set aside. Return skillet to stove and deglaze with white wine. Add garlic and rapini. Sauté for several minutes, then add shrimp. Continue to sauté until shrimp is cooked. Add tomatoes, pesto, ricotta and Romano cheese; remove from heat. Toss with fusilli and serve.

Park Plaza Hotel, Boston, MA

Pasta with Fresh Tuna

SERVES 4

8 ounces fresh tuna loin, cut into strips
4 cups fresh breadcrumbs
$1/2$ cup minced parsley
$1/4$ cup grated Romano cheese
3 tablespoons olive oil
$1/3$ cup minced onion
1 tablespoon minced garlic
3 anchovy fillets, minced
1 pound plum tomatoes, peeled, seeded, chopped
(or 1 large can chopped tomatoes, drained)
1 tablespoon capers
$1/4$ cup pitted green olives
1 pound elbow macaroni

SAUCE: Combine breadcrumbs, parsley and cheese in a small bowl. Set aside. Cut tuna into strips approximately $1/4$ inch by $1/4$ inch by $2^1/2$ inches and season lightly with pepper. Heat olive oil in a large skillet over medium heat. Add onion and garlic and sauté 3 minutes. Add anchovies and mash them with a wooden spoon until they "melt" into the garlic and onions. Add tomatoes. Cover partially and simmer 15 minutes. Raise heat to medium-high, add tuna and toss quickly, cooking until tuna is medium-rare. Stir in capers and olives, cook 30 seconds, cover and remove from heat. Taste and adjust seasoning as necessary.

TO SERVE: Cook pasta in a large pot of boiling water until just tender (8 to 10 minutes). Drain thoroughly and transfer to a warm serving bowl. Add half the breadcrumb mixture and toss well. Ladle sauce over top, then garnish with remaining breadcrumb mixture.

Certified Master Chef Michael Russell,
Motor City Casino, Detroit, MI

Smoked Salmon, Roasted Peppers & Penne in a Creamy Garlic Sauce

SERVES 10 AS A FIRST COURSE

6 ounces thinly sliced smoked salmon
2 large red bell peppers, cut in thin strips, 2 inches long
2 large green bell peppers, cut in thin strips, 2 inches long
1 small red onion, thinly sliced
1 cup olive oil
1 cup heavy cream
4 garlic cloves, crushed lightly
$1/4$ cup fresh lemon juice
2 tablespoons minced fresh dill
2 tablespoons minced fresh parsley
salt & pepper to taste
1 pound penne pasta

ROAST PEPPERS: Preheat oven to 475°. Toss peppers and onion with $1/4$ cup olive oil, season with salt. Roast peppers and onions for 10 minutes. Cool.

SAUCE: In a saucepan, bring cream to a boil over moderate heat. Add garlic, simmer 15 minutes, or until garlic is softened and cream is reduced to $1/2$ cup. In a blender or food processor purée mixture until it is very smooth. Add lemon juice and blend well. With motor running, add oil in a slow stream, blending mixture until it is emulsified. Blend in dill, parsley and salt & pepper to taste.

PASTA: Cook penne in boiling salted water until tender. While pasta is cooking, gently warm sauce. Drain pasta and transfer to a large serving bowl.

TO SERVE: Toss pasta with bell peppers, onion and smoked salmon, reserving 20 strips for garnish. Add sauce and toss gently. Divide among 10 salad plates and garnish each serving with 2 of the reserved salmon strips. Serve warm or at room temperature.

Sea Scallop Stir Fry with Sesame Noodles

*The next few recipes will satisfy cravings for
seafood with an Asian flair.*

SERVES 6

> 1 pound sea scallops
> $1/2$ cup chopped peanuts
> 1 bunch scallions, chopped
> 1 pound spaghetti, cooked

Dressing

> $1/2$ cup peanut butter
> $1/2$ cup tahini
> 3 tablespoons sesame oil
> 1 tablespoon hot chili oil
> 2 tablespoons rice wine vinegar
> 1 tablespoon grated ginger

Stir Fry

> 2 tablespoons peanut oil
> 1 teaspoon chopped fresh ginger
> $1/2$ teaspoon chopped garlic
> 1 bunch broccoli, chopped
> 1 can baby corn, drained
> $1/2$ pound snow pea pods, trimmed
> soy sauce to taste

NOODLES: Mix together dressing ingredients. Toss with spaghetti and peanuts. Garnish with scallions. Keep warm.

STIR FRY: Heat 1 tablespoon oil in wok. Add garlic and ginger. Stir fry for 1 minute. Add vegetables and keep turning in wok. Season with soy sauce. Cook until vegetables are just tender approximately 2-3 minutes. Remove vegetables from wok.

SCALLOPS: Add 1 tablespoon oil to wok. Add scallops and stir fry for 2-3 minutes.

TO SERVE: Once scallops are cooked, return vegetables to wok and combine. Serve over sesame noodles.

79

Curried Shrimp in Peanut Sauce

SERVES 4

$1^1/_2$ pounds large uncooked shrimp,
   peeled and deveined
8 ounces uncooked fettuccine
$^2/_3$ cup chicken broth
$^1/_2$ cup creamy peanut butter
2 tablespoons balsamic vinegar
1 piece peeled fresh ginger (about $^1/_2$-inch), thinly sliced
$^1/_2$ teaspoon salt
$^1/_8$ teaspoon black pepper
1 tablespoon olive oil
$1^1/_2$ cups sliced green onions
2 teaspoons curry powder
$1^1/_2$ teaspoons minced garlic
2 tablespoons chopped fresh cilantro

PASTA: Cook pasta according to package directions.

PEANUT SAUCE: Place broth, peanut butter, vinegar, ginger and salt & pepper in a blender or food processor, and process until smooth.

SHRIMP: Heat oil in a large non-stick skillet over medium heat. Add onions, curry, and garlic; sauté 3 minutes. Add shrimp; cook 6 minutes or until shrimp are done. Stir in peanut sauce; cook for 1 minute or until thoroughly heated.

TO SERVE: Toss pasta with shrimp and peanut sauce. Sprinkle with cilantro.

Hoisin Halibut with Vermicelli Noodles

SERVES 8

8 halibut steaks (1 inch thick, 6 ounces each)
$3/4$ pound vermicelli pasta
$1/4$ cup hoisin sauce, divided
3 tablespoons low-sodium soy sauce
1 tablespoon vegetable oil
1 tablespoon grated, peeled fresh ginger
1 cup sliced green onions
1 teaspoon chili paste
$1/2$ cup chicken broth
$1/8$ teaspoon fresh ground pepper
3 tablespoons rice vinegar
cooking spray

Preheat oven to 450°.

PASTA: Cook pasta according to package directions. Combine noodles, 2 tablespoons hoisin sauce and next 8 ingredients in a large bowl and keep warm.

HALIBUT: Rub fish with 2 tablespoons hoisin sauce. Place fish on a baking sheet coated with cooking spray. Bake for 10–12 minutes depending on thickness of the fillet. Turn heat to broil and finish cooking for 3 minutes.

TO SERVE: Place halibut portions over a bed of noodles.

Robert's Food Stores, North Madison, CT

81

Entrées

83

Entrée Recipes

Entrée Recipes (cont.)

86

ENTRÉES

87

Entrée Recipes (cont.)

SOFT-SHELL CRABS

*Blue crabs shed their hard shells during their annual molting
season, (generally May to September) and become soft-shell crabs!
A seasonal delicacy, soft-shell crabs are sold in varying sizes:
mediums, hotels, primes, jumbos and whales. Soft-shell crabs
must be cleaned before cooking.*

*To clean crabs: Cut away the eyes and mouth. Fold back one side
of the top shell, exposing the gills (gray-white & feathery looking).
Pull away and discard the gills from both sides of the crab.
Turn the crab over and fold back the tail flap, called the apron.
Pull the apron away from the body and discard.*

Grilled Soft-Shell Crabs

SERVES 4

**8 soft-shell crabs, cleaned
6 tablespoons butter, melted
3 tablespoons chopped garlic
salt & pepper**

Preheat grill to medium-hot. Mix together butter and chopped
garlic. Season cleaned crabs with salt and pepper, brush with
garlic butter and grill to brown on both sides, about 5–8 minutes
total. Brush again with garlic butter before serving.

Stuffed Soft-Shell Crabs with Golden Tomato Vinaigrette

SERVES 6

6 soft-shell crabs, cleaned
flour to dredge the crabs
Golden Tomato Vinaigrette
4 gold tomatoes, blanched, peeled and seeded
4 garlic cloves, minced fine
$1/2$ cup champagne vinegar
1 cup light olive oil
salt & pepper to taste
Stuffing
1 cup butter, melted (or salad oil)
1 Vidalia onion, sliced
4 cloves garlic, minced
$1/4$ cup minced fresh jalapeño
1 cup fresh breadcrumbs
$1/2$ cup chopped mixed fresh herbs (chives, parsley, basil and oregano)
salt & pepper
lemon juice
1 cup grated aged white cheddar

GOLDEN TOMATO VINAIGRETTE: Place tomatoes in a blender with garlic and vinegar. Pulse until smooth. With blender running, drizzle in olive oil. Season with salt and pepper.

STUFFING: Melt butter in saucepan. Add onions and cook until golden brown. Add garlic and chopped peppers. Cook until aromatic. Add breadcrumbs, herbs and season with salt, pepper and lemon juice. Let cool slightly. Fold in cheddar cheese. Refrigerate until cold.

CRABS: Stuff filling between soft-shell layer and body of cleaned crabs. Dredge stuffed crabs in flour. Heat approximately 2 inches of oil in a skillet on medium heat. Gently place crabs into oil. Cook until golden on both sides.

90

Serve immediately with a small ladle of Golden Tomato Vinaigrette.

Chef Casey Riley, Inn at Castle Hill, Newport, RI

Sautéed Soft-Shell Crabs

SERVES 2

4 soft-shell crabs, cleaned
salt & pepper
$1/2$ teaspoon lemon juice
paprika
flour for dredging
1 tablespoon chopped parsley
6 tablespoons butter
1 tablespoon dry vermouth
1 garlic clove, finely chopped

Season cleaned crabs on belly side with salt, pepper, lemon juice and paprika. Dredge lightly in flour. Sauté in 3 tablespoons butter, belly side down, for $2^{1}/2$ minutes then turn and sauté an additional $2^{1}/2$ minutes. Remove to hot platter. Melt remaining butter in pan. Add lemon juice, dry vermouth and garlic. When bubbling, pour over the crabs. Garnish with chopped parsley. Serve very hot.

Soft-Shell Crabs Sautéed with Almonds

SERVES 4

8–12 soft-shell crabs, cleaned
salt & pepper
flour
$1/2$ cup clarified butter
$1/2$ cup sliced, blanched almonds
juice of $1/2$ lemon
2 tablespoons chopped parsley

Preheat 2 large skillets. Season crabs, dip them in flour and shake excess off. Over medium heat, brown them in 4 tablespoons butter on both sides, approximately 3 minutes per side. Transfer to plates. Heat remaining butter in second pan. Add almonds and lightly brown. Stir in lemon juice and parsley. Spoon sauce over crabs.

Certified Master Chef Milos Cihelka (ret),
The Golden Mushroom, Detroit, MI

CRAB

At Foley's we favor Jonah crab harvested in the North Atlantic, primarily at the edge of the continental shelf. This crab is harvested year round and is known for the sweetness of its meat. Less well known than the Maryland blue crab, the Jonah crab tends to be more affordable and every bit as delicious. Jonah crab products are available fresh or frozen. We do not recommend using canned crab.

Foley Fish House Crab Cakes

SERVES 8 (16 CAKES)

These are so "crabby" they must be eaten with a fork!

2 pounds Jonah crabmeat
1 cup mayonnaise
2 teaspoons Old Bay® seasoning
$3/4$ teaspoon dry mustard
$2^1/2$ teaspoons lemon juice
$1/4$ teaspoon Tabasco
$1^1/4$ teaspoon Worcestershire sauce
$2^1/2$ teaspoons dry chives
$2/3$ cup panko (Japanese breadcrumbs)
1 cup white breadcrumbs

Preheat oven to 350°. Combine all ingredients. Form crab into cakes, approximately 3 inches in diameter. Place on a baking sheet and bake for 15-20 minutes or until golden brown.

*Chef Paul Weber, Foley Fish House,
Renaissance Hotel, Times Square, New York, NY*

Foley Fish House is located in the Renaissance Hotel in Times Square, New York City. Foley Fish does not own the restaurant; we simply provide the fresh seafood and lend our name. They have been a wonderful source of delicious recipes and these crab cakes are outstanding! Enjoy.

93

Pan-Fried Crabcakes on New England Brown Bread with Roast Corn Coulis

SERVES 4

Crabcakes

    4 medium scallops
    1 pound Jonah crabmeat, claw & knuckle
    2 tablespoons heavy cream
    $1/4$ cup roasted corn kernels ($1/2$ ear)
    $1/8$ cup roasted peppers, $1/4$-inch dice
    $1/8$ cup scallions, greens only, finely sliced
    salt & pepper
    $1/3$ cup fresh breadcrumbs
    3–4 tablespoons unsalted butter
    1 can B&M® Brown Bread with raisins
    $1/2$ bunch chives, finely chopped
    $1/3$ red bell pepper, finely diced

Roast Corn Coulis

    1 leek, washed well and roughly cut
    1 Spanish onion, peeled and finely sliced
    3 tablespoons unsalted butter
    $2^1/2$ cups roasted corn kernels ($2^1/2$ ears)
    1 cup chicken stock
    $3/4$ cup heavy cream
    salt & white pepper
    olive oil

TO ROAST CORN: Preheat oven to 475°. Brush ears of corn with olive oil and salt lightly. Place in oven for 8 minutes, rotating every 2 minutes to roast evenly. Remove from oven. Cool before removing kernels.

CRABCAKES: Purée scallops and cream in a food processor. Combine with crabmeat, corn, peppers and scallions in a mixing bowl. Mix thoroughly with a rubber spatula. Season with salt and pepper. Divide mixture into four $3^1/2$ ounce cakes, approximately $2^1/2$ inches across by 1 inch high. The

94

cakes should be circular. Coat cakes in breadcrumbs on all sides and refrigerate, covered.

ROAST CORN COULIS: Slowly cook leeks and onions with butter in a saucepan over medium heat. Stir and avoid coloring them. Add remaining ingredients and bring mixture to a boil. Place sauce mixture in a blender and process until smooth. Season with salt and white pepper. Keep hot in a double boiler until ready to serve.

PREPARATION: Preheat oven to 500°. Heat an ovenproof sauté pan over high heat and add butter to pan. Just before it begins to brown, add crabcakes, using a spatula. When cakes reach a golden brown color (approximately 1 minute), flip them and put the pan in the oven for about 5 minutes. They will be firm and hot in the center. Check by inserting tip of knife into center and removing — if knife tip is hot, cakes are done.

TO SERVE: Open the brown bread and cut four slices about 1/3 inch each. Cover four plates with Roast Corn Coulis. Place 1 slice of brown bread in the center of each plate. Remove cakes from oven and place one each on top of brown bread. Garnish the plate with chives and diced pepper. Serve immediately.

Chef Ted Gidley, Clarke Cooke House, Newport, RI

Mike Monahan's Crab Cakes

MAKES 10 CAKES

1 pound Jonah crabmeat
$1/2$ teaspoon Tabasco sauce
2 eggs, lightly beaten
1 tablespoon Dijon mustard
2 tablespoons mayonnaise
$1/2$ teaspoon chopped garlic
$1\ 1/2$ cups minced celery
1 tablespoon lemon juice
$1\ 1/2$ cups minced onion
1 teaspoon Worcestershire
1 teaspoon Old Bay Seasoning
1 teaspoon salt & pepper
1 cup fresh breadcrumbs
3 tablespoons butter
3 tablespoons canola oil

Preheat oven to 450°. Mix all ingredients and form into crab cakes. Heat 1 tablespoon butter and 1 tablespoon canola oil (per batch of cakes) in a 2 quart non-stick sauté pan. Sauté cakes for approximately 2 minutes per side or until golden brown. Finish in the oven for approximately 5 minutes or until heated through.

Monahan's Seafood Market, Ann Arbor, MI

CALAMARI/SQUID

Squid, or calamari as it is often called, is a very nutritious seafood offering—high in protein, low in fat and calories. To maintain its natural tenderness, squid should be cooked quickly or baked for an extended period of time. Squid is offered fresh or frozen— because it is a perishable product, frozen can be the best option. Most importantly, the squid you purchase should be 100 percent natural with no chemical additives. Squid is typically available in rings, tubes (which can be cut into rings) or tubes and tentacles.

Baked Stuffed Calamari with Italian Sauce

SERVES 6

$2^1/_2$ pounds calamari, tubes
   and tentacles, cleaned
melted butter
$1/_2$ cup red wine
Italian tomato sauce

Stuffing

1 tablespoon Parmesan cheese
2 cups fresh white breadcrumbs
1 small onion, chopped
2 garlic cloves, minced
tentacles, chopped fine
salt & pepper to taste
pinch of oregano
1 egg, lightly beaten

Preheat oven to 350°. Mix stuffing ingredients together with one beaten egg. Stuff squid tubes with mixture. Place in casserole. Paint with melted butter. Add red wine. Bake in oven for 15 minutes. Cover with Italian sauce and bake for another 30–45 minutes.

97

MUSSELS

Mussels are a delicious shellfish featuring a plump orange-yellow meat and blue to black shell. Mussels grow by attaching themselves by a "byssal thread" or "beard" to their environment. This beard should be removed just before cooking. Simply pull on the thread that is found at the hinge of the mussel where the two shells connect and remove. Mussels grow in sandy surroundings so feel free to rinse their shells before cooking.

Steamed Mussels

SERVES 4

3 dozen mussels
2 cups dry white wine
2 tablespoons olive oil
3 medium shallots, minced
2 garlic cloves, minced
1 teaspoon fresh thyme leaves or $1/2$ teaspoon dried
1 teaspoon salt
$1/2$ teaspoon pepper

Scrub and debeard mussels. In a large saucepan, combine wine, olive oil, shallots, garlic, thyme, salt and pepper. Bring to a boil over medium-high heat. Add mussels, cover and steam until mussels have opened, about 5 minutes. Discard any that do not open. Spoon out mussels with broth into individual serving bowls and serve at once.

Roche Brothers/Sudbury Farms, Boston, MA

98

Curried Mussels

SERVES 4

1 pound mussels, scrubbed and debearded
$1/4$ cup olive oil
1 large onion, finely chopped
3 garlic cloves, finely chopped
1 tablespoon curry powder
$1/4$ cup water
$1/4$ cup dry white wine
2 tablespoons chopped cilantro
pinch of salt
sliced French bread

Heat oil in Dutch oven over medium-high heat. Add onion and garlic and sauté until onion is translucent, about 8 minutes. Add curry powder and mix well.

Pour in water and wine. Increase heat to high and bring to boil. Add mussels, cover and steam until shells open, 3–6 minutes, shaking pan once or twice. Discard any mussels that do not open. Sprinkle with cilantro and salt. Spoon into shallow bowls. Serve mussels immediately with bread.

We like to think of mussels as social animals as their shells "gape" during storage as if they're chatting with each other. To be sure the mussel is still alive before cooking, simply hold it in your hand for a few seconds, if it closes, the mussel is still alive and okay to cook!

CLAMS

Clams come in all shapes and sizes depending on their habitat and species. Hard shell clams are quahogs and have different names depending on their size. Quahogs are the largest, then cherry-stones, topnecks, littlenecks and countneck clams. Smaller-sized hard shells are often served raw on the half-shell. Soft-shell or "steamer" clams are also popular. These clams have a thinner, more fragile shell, are oblong in shape and have a short, thin neck or "siphon" which protrudes from their shells. In New England soft-shells are steamed then served with butter and broth for dunking. They are a roll-up-your-sleeves summertime favorite!

Cheddar Quahog Fritters

MAKES 48 FRITTERS

1 pound chopped clams, drained
2 cups Vermont maple syrup
1 cup white wine
$1/2$ cup chopped Chipotle chilies, or to taste
2 cups sweet corn kernels
$1/4$ cup fresh orange juice
2 tablespoons fresh lemon juice

$1/2$ cup small white onion, finely diced
4 cloves garlic, minced
1 bunch scallions, diced
1 cup grated white cheddar cheese
$1/4$ cup chopped fresh basil
$1/4$ cup chopped fresh sage
15 eggs, yolks and whites separated
2–4 cups flour, as needed
salt & pepper
cayenne pepper to taste
Pinch cornstarch
1 tablespoon baking powder

MAPLE-CHIPOTLE SYRUP: Combine maple syrup and wine. Cook over medium heat until reduced by half. Cool and stir in chilies.

CLAMS: Place $2/3$ of corn kernels in a blender with orange juice, lemon juice, onion and garlic. Blend until very smooth. Place mixture in a bowl and add chopped clams, remaining corn kernels, scallions, herbs, cheese and egg yolks. Add flour 1 cup at a time, stirring until very thick ribbons develop. (Flour needed will vary based on wetness of mixture). Season with salt and peppers.

Preheat frying oil to 350°. In a mixer, whip 10 egg whites with pinch of salt and cornstarch to medium-soft peaks. Gently fold in egg whites, then baking powder. Drop by even spoonfuls into hot oil. Fry to dark golden brown, turning once. Drain.

Serve immediately with Maple-Chipotle Syrup.

Chef Casey Riley, Inn at Castle Hill, Newport, RI

Rance's Stuffed Quahogs

SERVES 15

30 quahogs
white wine
4 pounds sea scallops, diced
2 large onions, finely chopped
1 tablespoon butter
10 cups Ritz® cracker crumbs
3 cups Maître d'Hôtel Butter (see pg 190)
5 cups Italian breadcrumbs
2 green peppers, finely chopped
2 red peppers, finely chopped
2 tablespoons chopped jalapeños
Tabasco to taste

Place 2 cups water in a large saucepan with a splash of white wine. Add quahogs and steam over high heat until they open, approximately 5–8 minutes. Reserve 1 cup steaming liquid.

Remove meats, set aside and scrub all shells. Put meats in food processor and finely chop. Sauté onions in butter until translucent. Combine cracker crumbs with melted Maître d'Hôtel Butter, breadcrumbs, vegetables, Tabasco, scallop pieces, clam meats and clam juice.

Consistency should be moist but not watery; adjust with additional cracker crumbs if necessary.

Spoon generous portions of mixture into each shell. Place on a baking sheet with 1–2 tablespoons of water and bake for 20–25 minutes until golden brown.

NANTUCKET CAPE SCALLOPS

Somehow ... someway ... along the shore of the tiny island of Nantucket, when the stars align, the tidal currents are just right and the water temperature is perfect—the eel grass surrenders itself to become home to tiny scallop seedlings. These seedlings will grow into the most perfect scallop you will ever taste— the Nantucket Cape Scallop.

There are many bay scallops available but none are nearly as sweet, rich or tender as Nantucket Capes. Nantucket Cape Scallops are harvested annually between November and April. These scallops are best when prepared simply to allow their natural sweetness to shine. Nantucket Capes command a premium price but we believe they are worth every penny.

Baked Nantucket Cape Scallops

SERVES 4–6

$1^1/_2$ pounds Nantucket Cape scallops
2 tablespoons butter, melted
$^1/_2$ cup crushed Ritz crackers
1 tablespoon dry vermouth

Preheat oven to 450°. Place scallops in a baking dish. Melt butter and pour over scallops. Cover with a light coating of Ritz cracker crumbs and sprinkle with dry vermouth. Bake for 6-10 minutes.

103

Nantucket Cape Scallop Sauté

SERVES 4

1 pound Nantucket Cape scallops
2 tablespoons oil
2 tablespoons butter

Preheat non-stick sauté pan over medium-high heat. Add 1 tablespoon oil and 1 tablespoon butter. Add half the scallops and sear quickly for 1–2 minutes. Remove to warm platter. Add remaining oil and butter to pan and sear remaining scallops. Serve immediately.

There are typically between 40 and 60 Nantucket Cape scallops to a pound making one pound more than enough for 4 people. One pound will also serve 10 as a passed appetizer with each person getting between 4 and 6 scallops!

SEA SCALLOPS

*Many processors soak scallops to mask their inferior quality
and add false weight. If the scallops in your store are marked
"water added" or are bright white and have a jelly-like consistency,
they are soaked. Soaked scallops have no flavor and do not brown
when sautéed. Insist on fresh, all natural sea scallops. Sea scallops
are naturally creamy to tan in color with a sweet, ocean aroma.
They will brown in the pan, and feature a delicious, rich,
sweet flavor and firm texture.*

Sea Scallop Sauté with Fresh Herbs

SERVES 4

$1^1/_2$ pounds medium sea scallops (20–30 scallops)
salt & pepper
4 tablespoons clarified butter
$1/_2$ cup chopped fresh herbs (a combination of
   chives, parsley, tarragon, chervil)
zest of $1/_2$ lemon
1 tablespoon lemon juice
mashed potatoes

Preheat a large non-stick skillet. Season scallops with salt and
pepper. Add butter to hot pan, then add scallops in a single
layer. Sear scallops over high heat to heat through, about 2
minutes per side. Reduce heat slightly; add herbs, lemon zest
and juice; toss to coat. Serve hot with mashed potatoes.

*Certified Master Chef Milos Cihelka (ret),
Golden Mushroom, Southfield, MI*

Holiday Seafood Newburg

A Foley family holiday season tradition…
this will garner rave reviews!

SERVES 6–8

1 pound Jonah crabmeat
1 pound sea or bay scallops
1 pound cooked baby shrimp
4 ounces sliced mushrooms
$1/4$ cup + 2 tablespoons butter
1 can artichokes, drained, chopped
$1/4$ cup flour
$1/2$ teaspoon salt
dash of cayenne
$1^1/2$ cups half & half
1 cup sherry
2 tablespoons fresh breadcrumbs
1 tablespoon Parmesan cheese
paprika

Preheat oven to 450°.

SEAFOOD/ARTICHOKES/MUSHROOMS: Lightly sauté mushrooms in 1 tablespoon butter; set aside and keep warm. Add 1 tablespoon butter to pan and sauté seafood for 1 minute; set aside and keep warm. Place artichokes in bottom of a 2 quart casserole. Cover with mushrooms, then add seafood.

SAUCE: In saucepan, melt $1/4$ cup butter; whisk in flour and seasonings. Add cream gradually, cooking and stirring until thick. Stir in sherry. Heat through.

TO SERVE: Pour sauce over seafood in casserole. Combine breadcrumbs and Parmesan cheese. Sprinkle over top. Lightly sprinkle paprika over top of breadcrumb/Parmesan mixture. Bake for 12–15 minutes.

Pan-Seared Sea Scallops with Coconut Sauce & Rice

SERVES 4

> **1 pound medium sea scallops (20–30 scallops)**
> **salt & pepper to taste**
> **4 tablespoons olive oil**
> **1 tablespoon finely chopped shallots**
> **4 tablespoons Malibu Rum (or dry sherry)**
> **$1/2$ cup coconut milk**
> **1 cup heavy cream**
> **4 tablespoons butter**
> **cooked white or wild rice**

SCALLOPS: Season scallops with salt and pepper. Preheat sauté pan over medium-high heat. Add olive oil. Add scallops and sear for 3–4 minutes turning once. Remove scallops from pan and keep warm.

SAUCE: Add shallots to pan and sauté for 2 minutes over medium heat. Deglaze with Malibu Rum. Add coconut milk and heavy cream; cook over medium heat until reduced by half. Add cooked scallops to coconut milk and heavy cream. Whisk in butter, stirring until fully melted.

TO SERVE: Serve atop white or white/wild rice combination.

Bally's Grand Casino, Atlantic City, NJ

Pan-Seared Sea Scallops with Italian Greens & Rosemary Sauce

SERVES 4

1 pound sea scallops (40 small scallops or 20 large)
1 bunch broccoli rabe, washed and stemmed
4 tablespoons extra virgin olive oil
2 tablespoons minced garlic
1 28-ounce can chopped tomatoes, drained
1 tablespoon fresh rosemary, chopped

Cook broccoli rabe in boiling water for 3–5 minutes. Drain. Preheat non-stick sauté pan over high heat. Add scallops and pan sear over high heat for 2–3 minutes. Remove from pan and keep warm. In same pan, add 2 tablespoons olive oil and sauté garlic until soft but not brown. Add tomatoes and rosemary. Season to taste.

Return scallops to pan, heat through and serve atop hot broccoli rabe.

Robert's Food Stores, North Madison, CT

Sea Scallops in Foil

SERVES 8

**2 pounds sea scallops
8 shallots, minced
3 large tomatoes, diced
1 large fennel bulb, thinly sliced
4 tablespoons olive oil
1 teaspoon salt
$1/2$ teaspoon fresh ground pepper
1 cup + 4 tablespoons butter
$1/2$ cup minced fresh basil
grated peel of 1 lemon
aluminum foil**

Preheat oven to 400°.

SAUCE: In a large skillet over medium heat, sauté shallots, tomatoes and fennel in oil until most of liquid is absorbed, about 3 minutes; season with salt and pepper. Set aside to cool.

TO ASSEMBLE: Cut 8 squares of aluminum foil, about 10x10 inches each. Smear each with 2 tablespoons butter. Place an equal amount of tomato/fennel mixture in center of each foil square. Place $1/4$ pound scallops on tomato/fennel mixture. Cut any very large scallops so they will cook evenly. Place 1 tablespoon basil on each mound of scallops, top with $1 1/2$ teaspoons butter and $1/2$ teaspoon lemon peel. Seal foil packages securely. Refrigerate if not baking immediately.

TO SERVE: Place packages on a baking sheet and bake until packages puff, about 12–14 minutes, depending on size of scallops. Place a package on each dinner plate and open at the table so the aroma can be enjoyed.

*Certified Master Chef Michael Russell,
Motor City Casino, Detroit, MI*

109

Ginger-Seared Sea Scallops with Braised Bok Choy

SERVES 4–6

2 pounds sea scallops
$1/2$ cup white wine
$1/4$ cup low-sodium soy sauce
$1/4$ cup olive oil
6 tablespoons ginger, peeled and finely diced
1 tablespoon chopped chives
cracked pepper
$1/4$ pound pancetta, diced (may substitute bacon)
1 pound baby bok choy, thinly sliced
$1/4$ cup zinfandel

MARINADE: Combine white wine, soy sauce, 2 tablespoons olive oil, ginger, chives and cracked pepper. Add scallops and marinate, refrigerated, for one hour.

BOK CHOY: Heat a sauté pan and cook pancetta until crisp. Add bok choy to pan and toss. Cook over high heat for two minutes and then deglaze with zinfandel. Reduce liquid until gone. Set aside bok choy in a warm place.

TO SERVE: Sear scallops in 2 tablespoons olive oil in a hot sauté pan, browning on each side. Cook until slightly warm in the center, about 2 minutes per side. Deglaze pan with some of the marinade. Cook for a minute longer. Serve over braised bok choy.

Chef Joe Rebas (ret), Parker House, Boston, MA

110

SHRIMP

Shrimp can be confusing because there are so many varieties available. At Foley's we prefer Mexican, #1 grade shrimp for its superb flavor. Most shrimp have been previously frozen, unless you are lucky enough to live in a port that lands local fresh shrimp. The most important thing when purchasing shrimp is to ensure that it is 100 percent natural with no chemical preservatives that will interfere with the flavor and cause a jelly-like consistency.

Shrimp Scampi à la Scotty

SERVES 4

16 large shrimp, peeled and deveined
Marinade
$1/2$ **cup olive oil**
$1/2$ **teaspoon salt**
$1/2$ **teaspoon fresh ground pepper**
2 garlic cloves, chopped fine
$1/4$ **cup butter**
juice of 1 lemon
2 tablespoons chopped Italian parsley
$1/4$ **cup dry vermouth**

Marinate shrimp in refrigerator for 1 hour. Place 4 tablespoons marinade in sauté pan over medium-high heat. Sauté shrimp for 2 minutes on each side. Add 2 more garlic cloves, if desired. Add butter, lemon juice, parsley and dry vermouth to pan. Blend together and cook for approximately 5 more minutes. Serve hot.

Spicy Shrimp with Citrus Salsa

SERVES 10

30 – 16/20 count shrimp, peeled & deveined
$1/4$ cup white wine
2 tablespoons olive oil
1 tablespoon chopped garlic
1 tablespoon chopped shallots
juice of 2 lemons
juice of 2 limes
1 tablespoon chopped fresh rosemary
1 tablespoon chopped fresh thyme
1 teaspoon cayenne pepper
salt & pepper
4 tablespoons unsalted butter

Citrus Salsa (make 1 day ahead)
2 ruby grapefruit, peeled and seeded
3 oranges, peeled and seeded
4 lemons, peeled and seeded
4 limes, peeled and seeded
2 kiwi fruit, peeled and cut into thin wedges
$1/4$ cup hot cherry peppers, seeded
1 red pepper, diced
$1/2$ bunch cilantro, chopped
1 yellow pepper, diced
$1/4$ cup diced leeks

SALSA: Place in a bowl: grapefruit, orange, lemon and lime segments with pith and membrane removed. Squeeze juice from skins and membrane into the bowl. Add kiwi. Purée hot cherry peppers and add. Add remaining ingredients and marinate overnight.

SHRIMP: Combine white wine, olive oil, garlic, shallots, citrus juices, herbs and seasoning to make a marinade. Marinate shrimp for 2–3 hours. Heat sauté pan. Add olive oil and then shrimp. Sear shrimp quickly. Deglaze pan with white wine and simmer until shrimp is cooked through. Add butter and toss.

TO SERVE: Divide salsa among 10 plates; arrange shrimp on top.

Chef Joe Rebas (ret), The Parker House, Boston, MA

Jamaican Shrimp & Scallops

SERVES 4–6

1 pound jumbo shrimp, peeled and deveined
$1/2$ pound sea scallops
salt & pepper to taste
1/4 teaspoon Old Bay seasoning
2 tablespoons extra-virgin olive oil
2 tablespoons unsalted butter
1 small onion, finely chopped
1 small plum tomato, diced
2 teaspoons mild Indian curry powder
$1/2$ cup chicken stock
1 tablespoon heavy cream
1 sprig fresh thyme
$1/2$ jalapeño or habanero chili pepper

SHRIMP AND SCALLOPS: Season shrimp and scallops with salt, pepper and Old Bay seasoning. Heat olive oil in a skillet over medium heat. Placing no more than 3 or 4 pieces in the pan at a time, cook seafood in hot oil until just cooked through, about 2 or 3 minutes on each side. Transfer cooked seafood to a platter and keep warm.

SAUCE: Melt butter over medium heat and sauté onion and tomato until onion softens, about 4 minutes. Add curry powder and cook, stirring, for 2 minutes. Add chicken stock, stir and let mixture simmer for 1 minute. Pour mixture into a blender and purée until smooth. Add heavy cream and pulse a few times just to blend in cream. Pour sauce back into a skillet over low heat and add sprig of thyme and chili pepper, if desired. Let cook for 3–4 minutes, then taste and adjust seasonings.

TO SERVE: Drizzle sauce over seafood and serve.

Shrimp & Scallop Skewers Brushed with Cajun Butter

SERVES 10

20 medium sea scallops
20 thawed jumbo shrimp, peeled and deveined
3 lemons, cut into thick slices
2 large red bell peppers, divided into 10 pieces
10 large white button mushrooms
10 wooden skewers, soaked overnight,
   or greased metal skewers

Cajun Butter

16 garlic cloves, peeled
4 shallots, peeled
$1/2$ cup chopped fresh basil
2 tablespoons fresh thyme leaves
3 sticks unsalted butter
2 tablespoons Worcestershire sauce
1 teaspoon salt
1 teaspoon black pepper
1 teaspoon white pepper
$1/2$ teaspoon cayenne pepper

SKEWERS: Thread skewers in this order: scallop, lemon, shrimp, pepper, shrimp, mushroom, scallop.

CAJUN BUTTER: In food processor, mince garlic and shallots; add basil and thyme and mince again. Add remaining ingredients and process until smooth. Transfer to a small bowl. (May cover and refrigerate up to 8 hours in advance.)

GRILLING: Just before grilling, transfer Cajun Butter to a small saucepan and melt over low heat. Brush on skewers prior to grilling. Grill skewers over medium-hot coals or on a medium setting for 10 minutes or until shrimp are bright pink. Turn skewers often and baste frequently with melted Cajun Butter.

LOBSTER

Our favorite lobsters are hard-shell cold water lobsters from Maine and Nova Scotia. The sweet, tender meat fills the shell beautifully, making for an extravagant feast!

Boiled Lobster

Serves 4–6
4–6 lobsters, (1 to 1$^1/_2$ pounds each)
salt
lemon wedges
melted butter

Fill a 5-gallon pot halfway with water, add salt and bring to a boil. Drop in lobsters upside down; cover and reduce heat below simmer. Cook 15 minutes for one-pounders; add 3 minutes for every half pound heavier. When done, remove from water. Pull off arms with claws and crack them using a heavy, flat object. Using a large knife, split bodies into halves, lengthwise. Remove the stomach (a small sack between the eyes) and the intestinal vein in the tail and discard. Keep the liver (soft green matter) called tomalley, which is considered a delicacy. Serve lobsters with lemon and melted butter.

Lobster Newburg

SERVES 2–4

1 pound cooked lobster meat
$1/3$ cup butter
3 tablespoons flour
dash of cayenne
$1/2$ teaspoon salt
$1/2$ teaspoon paprika
$1 1/2$ cups light cream
3 egg yolks, beaten
4 tablespoons sherry
toast points or patty shells

Remove any shells or cartilage from lobster meat. Melt butter. Blend in flour and seasonings. Add cream and egg yolks gradually; cook until thick and smooth, stirring constantly. Add lobster meat; heat. Remove from heat and slowly stir in sherry. Serve immediately on toast points or patty shells.

> During the 1800's lobsters in America were so plentiful they were used as bait for striped bass and cod.

117

COD

Cod's glistening, moist white flakes and mild, sweet flavor have made it a favorite for generations. The term scrod is often used interchangeably with cod on menus across the country. Scrod means "small" and is used at fish auctions to distinguish small cod — "scrod" cod from larger cod — "market" cod.

Foley customers have coined the term "cod cousins" to refer to fish which have characteristics very similar to cod. We have included recipes for cod cousins hake, haddock and pollock. "Cousin" recipes can be used interchangeably for any of the "cousin" species.

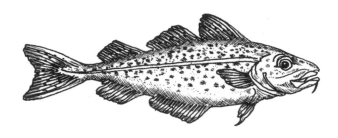

Foley's Baked Cod

SERVES 4

$1^1/_2$ pounds cod fillets
2 tablespoons melted butter
1 cup crushed Ritz crackers
2 tablespoons water

Preheat oven to 450°. Divide fillets into 4 portions. Lightly coat fillets with butter and dredge in cracker crumbs. Put fillets in a baking pan. Add 1-2 tablespoons water to pan to humidify the oven. Bake for 10 minutes per inch of thickness.

Note: For a spicier treat, spread Dijon mustard on the fish before dredging in cracker crumbs.

Cod with Tomato & Artichoke Sauce

SERVES 4

4 cod fillets (6 ounces each)
2 tablespoons olive oil
1 small onion, chopped
3 large garlic cloves, chopped
1 14-ounce can artichoke hearts, drained, chopped
$1^1/_2$ teaspoons dried oregano
1 28-ounce can diced tomatoes, (reserve juice)
salt & pepper

Heat oil in large, heavy skillet over medium heat. Add onion and garlic. Sauté until onion is almost tender, about 3 minutes. Add artichokes and oregano. Sauté for about 3 minutes. Stir in tomatoes and reserved juice and bring to a boil. Season fish with salt and pepper. Place fish atop vegetables in skillet. Cover skillet and reduce heat to medium-low. Simmer until fish is just opaque in center, about 5 minutes. Transfer fish to platter; keep warm.

Increase heat under pan and boil mixture in skillet until liquid thickens to sauce consistency, about 5 minutes. Season with salt and pepper. Serve fish with sauce over the top.

Mushroom-Crusted Cod

SERVES 6

3 pounds cod fillets
2 shallots, coarsely chopped
2 sticks cold butter
1 cup fresh mushrooms, sliced
salt & pepper
2 tablespoons chopped fresh parsley
2 teaspoons chopped fresh marjoram
$1/2$ teaspoon chopped fresh thyme
$1/4$ cup panko (Japanese breadcrumbs)
flour

Preheat oven to 400°.

MUSHROOM CRUST: Sauté shallots in 2 tablespoons of butter for 1 minute. Add mushrooms, salt & pepper and continue to sauté until mushrooms are almost completely cooked. Remove mushroom mixture from pan and allow to cool in refrigerator. When cool, finely chop mushroom mixture. Dice remaining butter into $1/2$-inch cubes and place in mixer. Whip butter until smooth. Add chopped mushroom mixture, herbs and breadcrumbs and blend thoroughly. Season to taste.

COD: Spread a $1/3$-inch layer of mushroom mixture on each cod portion. Lightly dust the top of each portion with flour. In a hot pan, sauté cod, crust side down until crust is set and lightly browned, approximately 1 minute. Flip portions and place on a sheet pan. Bake until done, approximately 3–6 minutes.

Neal Corman, Shaw's Crab House, Deerfield, IL

Cod with Chanterelles & Sherry Cream

This was served to President Clinton when he visited the Sherwood Inn.

SERVES 2

2 cod fillets (8 ounces each)
1 tablespoon butter
1 tablespoon olive oil
salt & pepper
2 cups sliced chanterelle mushrooms
2 tablespoons chopped shallots
1 cup sherry wine
1 cup chicken stock
$1/2$ cup heavy cream
2 cups mashed potatoes
2 tablespoons chopped chives

Preheat oven to 450°.

COD: Melt butter and olive oil in heavy-bottomed, oven-proof sauté pan over medium heat. Season cod with salt and pepper. When butter froths, add cod, presentation side down. After 2–3 minutes, put pan with fish in a 450° oven (do not flip fish). When fish is done, about 5–10 minutes depending on thickness, remove from pan and flip onto paper towel to rest.

SAUCE: Return pan to stove, add a pat of butter and chanterelle mushrooms; sauté for 2–3 minutes. Add shallots and sauté for 2–3 more minutes. Deglaze pan with sherry and ignite to flame. Add chicken stock and reduce until it coats the back of a spoon. Add cream and season with salt and pepper.

TO SERVE: Place cod browned side up on top of mashed potatoes. Spoon chanterelle mushrooms and sauce around the outside of the plate. Garnish with chives.

Chef Chris Kuhn, Sherwood Inn, Skaneateles, NY

Pan-Seared Codfish with Crab Sauce

SERVES 2

Crab Sauce

> 6 ounces fresh crabmeat
> 1 small onion diced
> 1 small carrot, diced
> 2 sprigs fresh thyme
> 2 tablespoons vegetable oil
> $1/4$ cup dry sherry
> $2/3$ cup heavy cream
> 1 teaspoon tomato paste
> salt and white pepper to taste

Cod

> 2 skinless cod fillets (8 ounces each)
> 1 tablespoon canola oil
> 2 teaspoons chopped fresh parsley
> $1/2$ teaspoon salt
> $1/4$ teaspoon ground black pepper
> 2 teaspoons extra virgin olive oil
> fresh chives, chopped

CRAB SAUCE: In a large, heavy saucepan, sauté diced vegetables and thyme in oil until onions begin to brown. Pour in sherry and deglaze pan. Simmer until volume is reduced by half. Add heavy cream and bring just to the boiling point. Immediately reduce heat to medium and continue cooking to reduce by one third. Add tomato paste and mix well. Add crabmeat and heat through. Add salt and white pepper to taste.

COD: Heat a heavy skillet over high heat. Add canola oil. Combine parsley, salt and pepper. Drizzle olive oil on top of fish and sprinkle with parsley mixture. Place seasoned fish parsley side down into hot pan. Reduce heat to medium-high and cook for 3–4 minutes. Turn fillets and cook for an additional 4 minutes.

Garnish with chives and serve with Crab Sauce.

Lime-Glazed Cod Fillets

SERVES 4

$1^1/_2$ pounds cod fillets
cooking spray
1 tablespoon lime juice
1 tablespoon light mayonnaise
$^1/_8$ teaspoon onion powder
$^1/_8$ teaspoon black pepper
$^1/_2$ cup seasoned breadcrumbs
$1^1/_2$ tablespoons melted butter
2 tablespoons chopped fresh parsley

Preheat oven to 450°. Place fish in an 11x7 baking dish coated with cooking spray. Combine lime juice, mayonnaise, onion powder and pepper in a small bowl. Spread over fish. Sprinkle with breadcrumbs; drizzle with butter. Add 1–2 tablespoons water to baking pan to humidify oven. Bake for 10 minutes per inch of thickness or until fish flakes easily when tested with a fork. Sprinkle with parsley and serve.

We believe the best cod, haddock, flounder and scallops are those harvested from an area called Georges Bank, located approximately 120 miles off the coast of Cape Cod. The Georges Bank is a nutrient-rich fishing ground where tidal currents converge to create upwellings bringing great amounts of fish food to the species that reside there. The fish harvested here are sweeter and "meatier" than those harvested from other fishing grounds.

Vegetable-Topped Cod Loin

SERVES 4–6

4–6 cod fillets (8 ounces each;
   thicker fillets preferable)
sea salt & white pepper
flour
3 tablespoons olive oil
2 tablespoons white wine
$1/4$ cup chicken stock

Vegetable Topping

4 tablespoons olive oil
$1/2$ cup minced Vidalia onion
$1/2$ cup minced carrot
$1/2$ cup minced celery
$1/2$ cup minced, peeled eggplant
$1/2$ cup minced zucchini
$1/2$ cup minced peeled, seeded tomato
$1/2$ cup panko (Japanese breadcrumbs)
1 tablespoon parsley
1 teaspoon dried thyme
salt & pepper

VEGETABLE TOPPING: Cook each vegetable separately with a little olive oil over low heat until tender and any liquid has evaporated. Combine in a bowl with seasoning, crumbs and herbs.

COD: Preheat oven to 450°. Season fish and dust lightly with flour. Sear in olive oil in an ovenproof sauté pan until crusted. Flip over and add wine and stock to pan. Top with vegetables and finish in oven for 6-8 minutes.

*Chef Anthony Spinella, Atlantic City Hilton,
Atlantic City, NJ*

Horseradish-Crusted Cod

Serve this when you want to "wow" your guests.

SERVES 4

4 cod fillets (6 ounces each)
1 cup mayonnaise
$1/2$ cup prepared horseradish
1 tablespoon chopped dill
salt & pepper
seasoned flour
2 cups fresh breadcrumbs
canola oil for frying
$1/2$ cup olive oil
$1/2$ cup chopped shallots
4 tablespoons sweet butter
2 tablespoons flour
$1/2$ cup white wine
$1/2$ cup chicken or fish stock (see page 54)
$1/2$ cup aged balsamic vinegar

COD: Combine mayonnaise, horseradish, dill and salt & pepper. Dredge cod fillets in seasoned flour, shake off excess. Dip in horseradish mixture to coat lightly. Place coated fillets in breadcrumbs and press firmly to coat. Sauté cod in $1/4$ inch of oil over medium-high heat until crisp and golden on both sides, about 4 minutes per side.

SAUCE: Caramelize shallots in olive oil in a small sauté pan. In another pan, make a roux by melting butter and whisking in flour until there are no lumps. Cook over low heat for 10 minutes. Meanwhile, bring wine, stock and vinegar to a boil. Once roux is complete, whisk in wine mixture. Continue whisking until completely incorporated. Add caramelized shallots. Season with salt and pepper; keep warm. When cod is finished, ladle $1/4$ cup of sauce onto each plate and top with cod. Simon Pearce serves this over mashed potatoes.

Executive Chef Rob Newton, Simon Pearce, Quechee, VT

125

Roasted Cod with Spicy Crab Crust

SERVES 4

Cod

> 4 cod portions (6 ounces each,
>   thick fillets work best)
> salt & fresh ground pepper
> 4 tablespoons olive oil
> $1/2$ pound fresh spinach, stemmed, washed, dried
> chopped fresh chives

Sauce

> 2 red bell peppers
> 4 peeled garlic cloves
> olive oil
> $1/2$ cup chicken or fish stock (see page 54)
> salt and fresh ground pepper

Crab Crust

> $1/2$ pound crabmeat, picked over to remove cartilage
> 2 tablespoons chopped chives
> 2 tablespoons mayonnaise
> 1 large egg, beaten lightly
> 1 teaspoon Old Bay seasoning
> $1/2$ teaspoon baking powder
> 3–4 drops Tabasco

SAUCE: Preheat oven to 400°. Rub peppers and garlic lightly with olive oil and roast them in a small roasting pan until peppers are softened and the skins are lightly charred, about 20 minutes. Cool completely; scrape seeds and skins from peppers. In blender on high speed, purée peppers and garlic until smooth, adding enough stock to make a sauce of thick pouring consistency. Season with salt and pepper to taste.

CRUST: In a small bowl, beat chives, mayonnaise, egg, Old Bay, baking powder and Tabasco until blended. Gently fold in the crab.

COD: Pat cod dry with paper towels. Season both sides with salt and pepper. In a large skillet heat 2 tablespoons of oil over medium-high heat. Add cod and cook until underside is lightly browned, about 3 minutes. Remove cod from skillet and place brown side down on broiler pan. Preheat broiler. Top cod evenly with crab mixture and broil 4 inches from heat until golden brown, about 6–8 minutes.

SPINACH: While cod is broiling, heat remaining oil in large skillet over medium heat. Add spinach and sauté quickly. Season to taste with salt and pepper. Divide spinach among 4 plates and top with a piece of cod. Drizzle with sauce and garnish with chives.

Chef Tim Mullen, Windows,
Renaissance Harborplace, Baltimore, MD

HADDOCK

Haddock is the fish that many New Englanders ate weekly until it became scarce and expensive due to overfishing. Happily, haddock has enjoyed a wonderful comeback thanks to strict fishery management measures. Haddock is very similar to cod yet a bit firmer, lending itself to a variety of preparation styles. Haddock is often sold with the skin on to distinguish it from cod—look for the black lateral line on the skin side to be sure you are getting authentic haddock.

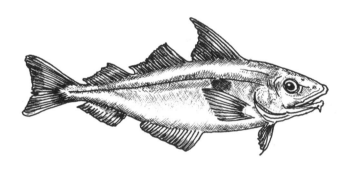

Haddock with Bacon Basil Pesto

SERVES 4

2 pounds haddock fillets
2 cloves garlic, chopped
$1/4$ cup cooked and crumbled thick-cut bacon
1 loaf of soft bread
1 cup fresh basil leaves
$1/4$ cup fresh parsley tops
1 cup olive oil
$1/2$ cup canola oil

Preheat oven to 450°. Combine garlic, bacon and bread in food processor; process to combine. Add greens, process again. Slowly drizzle in oils and process to combine. Place haddock fillets in baking pan and top with pesto. Bake for 10 minutes per inch of thickness.

Chef Kerry Romainello,
Westport Rivers Vineyard, Westport, MA

Cornmeal-Crusted Haddock with Black Bean Salsa

SERVES 4

1¹/₂ pounds haddock fillets, skinned
1 quart buttermilk
1 cup coarse cornmeal
Black Bean Salsa
2 avocados, peeled and coarsely chopped
salt
10 cherry tomatoes, quartered
3 tablespoons chopped cilantro
1 10-ounce can black beans, drained & rinsed
olive oil
¹/₂ red onion, minced
zest and juice of 1 lime

BLACK BEAN SALSA: Mix all ingredients together, set aside at room temperature.

HADDOCK: Preheat oven to 450°. Soak skinned haddock in buttermilk for ¹/₂ hour. Drain. Slice haddock into portions. Roll each portion in cornmeal. Coat cast iron pan with 1 tablespoon oil. Heat over high heat and sear haddock on each side to brown, approximately 2 minutes per side. Finish haddock in oven for 6-8 minutes. Serve with Black Bean Salsa.

Chef Kerry Romainello,
Westport Rivers Vineyard, Westport, MA

Bill's Favorite Haddock

SERVES 4

1 pound haddock, cut into 4 portions
2 tablespoons butter
2 tablespoons all purpose flour
$1^1/_4$ cups warm milk
$1/_4$ cup firmly packed, grated, sharp white cheddar cheese
dash of Worcestershire sauce
sherry, to taste
salt and white pepper to taste

Preheat oven to 450°.

SAUCE: In a medium saucepan, melt butter then stir in flour. Cook uncovered over medium-low heat, stirring occasionally, until the roux is fragrant, but not darkened, about 2–3 minutes. Remove from heat and let cool slightly. Slowly whisk warm milk into the roux and return to heat. Bring sauce slowly to simmer, whisking to prevent lumps and skimming any skin that forms on the surface. Continue cooking over low heat until sauce reaches the consistency of thick cream soup, about 8–10 minutes. Add cheese to sauce, stirring, just until the cheese is melted. Add Worcestershire sauce, sherry and season to taste with salt and pepper. Should the sauce become stringy, bring it just to a simmer and whisk in a few drops of white wine or lemon juice, then remove from the heat.

HADDOCK: Spoon some of the sauce into a oven-proof baking dish and arrange the haddock portions on top but not allowing them to touch. Spoon remaining sauce over the haddock. Bake for 10 minutes then brown under the broiler for 2–3 minutes.

Haddock with Tomato Sauce

SERVES 4

4 portions haddock (8 ounces each)
salt
flour
6 tablespoons olive oil
2 cloves of garlic, crushed
14-ounce can peeled & seeded chopped tomatoes
2 bay leaves
1 bunch of parsley, chopped finely

HADDOCK: Salt and flour haddock portions. Fry haddock in 4 tablespoons of very hot oil until lightly golden, about 1–2 minutes each side. Drain haddock on paper towels and set aside.

TOMATO SAUCE: Heat remaining oil in a large sauté pan. Add garlic and cook over low heat for 2–3 minutes. Add tomatoes and bay leaves. Bring to simmer, stirring occasionally, until liquid is reduced. Nestle haddock into pan among the tomatoes. Add the parsley. Cook for 5–8 minutes. Discard the bay leaves and serve hot.

Note: To use recipe as a sauce for pasta or rice, double the tomato quantity and flake fish at the end of cooking.

HAKE

Hake is a "cod cousin" that is harvested from the Gulf of Maine. Hake is a relatively unknown species so it is often more affordable than its other cousins. Hake is white-fleshed, mild-flavored, flaky and extremely moist.

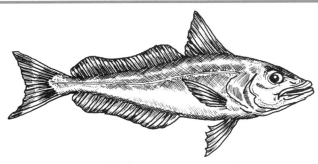

Hake with Tomato Basil Sauce

SERVES 4

4 hake fillets (about 6 ounces each)
olive oil
2 tablespoons chopped garlic
4 chopped scallions
4 large tomatoes, seeded, chopped
2 tablespoons basil
4 tablespoons white wine
salt & pepper to taste
flour

TOMATO BASIL SAUCE: Preheat pan over low heat. Add 1 tablespoon olive oil and garlic. Sauté garlic 2–3 minutes. Add scallions, tomatoes, basil and wine. Simmer for 8–10 minutes or until cooked through. Season to taste. Keep warm.

HAKE: Lightly coat fillets with flour. Heat pan over high heat. Add olive oil. Sauté hake quickly in olive oil until both sides are brown, approximately 4 minutes per side. Remove from pan. Serve Tomato Basil Sauce over fish.

Sesame Hake with Lemon Chive Sauce

SERVES 4

4 hake fillets (about 6 ounces each)

Coating

1 cup sesame seeds

1 cup grated Parmesan cheese

1 cup fresh breadcrumbs

flour

egg wash (1 egg, slightly beaten together with $^1/_2$ cup milk)

canola oil

Lemon Chive Sauce

$^1/_2$ cup white wine

1 tablespoon chopped shallots

2 tablespoons chopped chives

1 tablespoon chopped parsley

1 tablespoon lemon juice

$^3/_4$ cup butter, cut into small pieces

HAKE: Preheat oven to 400°. Mix sesame seeds, Parmesan cheese and breadcrumbs together. Dredge fillets in flour, dip in egg wash and roll in breadcrumb mixture. Heat $^1/_4$ inch canola oil in large sauté pan. Brown each side of hake fillets in oil then remove to a non-stick baking sheet. Bake for 8–10 minutes.

LEMON CHIVE SAUCE: While hake is baking, add wine to a sauté pan and reduce by half. Add shallots, chives, parsley and lemon juice. After sauce has blended, remove from heat and swirl in butter.

TO SERVE: Remove hake from oven and top with Lemon Chive Sauce.

ATLANTIC POLLOCK

Atlantic pollock has been an under-appreciated species due to its slightly darker hued flesh. In fact, when cooked, Atlantic Pollock is light and flaky. Its slightly higher oil content gives it a somewhat richer flavor than other white fish fillets. Pollock is also a firmer fish making it a best bet for soups and chowders.

Lemon Pollock

SERVES 4

1 pound pollock
 fillets, cut into
 4 portions
2 shallots
1 bunch of parsley, plus additional for garnish
1 lemon, cut in half
$1/2$ cup white wine
1 sprig dill plus dill for garnish
breadcrumbs as needed
1 tablespoon capers
salt & pepper to taste

Preheat oven to 450°. Chop shallots and parsley together. Squeeze half of lemon, reserve juice. Peel other half, slice thin.

Add wine, lemon juice, shallots, parsley, dill and fish to an oven-proof pan. Top with lemon slices. Place on a burner and bring liquid to a fast boil for 1 minute. Transfer pan to oven and cook for 10 minutes per inch of thickness of fish. When fish is cooked, place it on a hot serving plate; keep warm.

Return pan to burner and bring remaining liquid to a fast boil, adding just enough breadcrumbs to thicken. Add capers, discard dill. Pour sauce atop the fish and garnish with fresh parsley leaves, more fresh dill and remaining lemon slices.

134

FLOUNDER/SOLE

Flounder is almost always referred to as "sole" on menus and in markets. In the Northeast, there are a variety of different flounders—winter flounder, witch flounder, summer flounder— but most are sold as generic "flounder" or "sole." Whatever the terminology in your local store, flounders from the North Atlantic are light, flaky, delicate and delicious. They are best prepared either sautéed or rolled and stuffed.

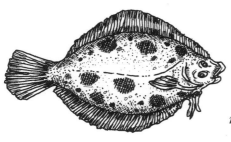

This Sole Rocks

This recipe converted even the most ardent "non-fish" eaters in the Foley office.

SERVES 2

4–6 sole/flounder fillets (4–6 ounces each)
4 tablespoons oil
$1/4$ cup pine nuts
2 tablespoons fresh basil, cut into strips
1 cup chopped tomatoes
flour for dredging

SAUCE: Preheat pan over medium-high heat. Heat 1 tablespoon of oil in frying pan, and toast pine nuts until light brown and fragrant. Lower heat, add basil and chopped tomatoes to pan. Cook until tomatoes break down; set aside.

FISH: Lightly dredge sole in flour. Preheat sauté pan over high heat. Add oil. Lightly sauté fish over medium-high heat 2 minutes on first side, and 1 minute on second. Salt and pepper to taste.

TO SERVE: Spoon sauce over sole and garnish with basil.

Georges Bank Sole Wellington

SERVES 8

**16 small sole/flounder fillets (2–4-ounce fillets)
1 pound cooked baby shrimp
1 cup Jonah crabmeat
3 tablespoons chopped shallots
1 tablespoon chopped garlic
2 tablespoons butter
2 cups sliced mushrooms
flour
$1/2$ cup white wine
2 cups heavy cream
salt & pepper
$1/4$ cup fresh Parmesan cheese, grated
1 tablespoon Pernod
2 puff pastry sheets, cut in quarters**

Preheat oven to 400°.

SEAFOOD STUFFING: Sauté shallots and garlic in butter. Add mushrooms. Cook for 2–3 minutes. Add shrimp and heat through. Remove from pan and combine with crabmeat. Dust seafood mixture with flour and return to pan and sauté for 2–3 minutes. Add wine and heavy cream and simmer until cream thickens. Season with salt and pepper, Parmesan and Pernod. Let mixture cool. Form into balls.

SOLE: Lay 2 pieces of sole side by side and roll them around stuffing. Meanwhile, roll out one quarter of a puff pastry sheet. Wrap this around the sole. Repeat for each sole/stuffing portion. Bake for 15 minutes or until pastry is golden brown.

Note: Pastry may be brushed with egg white $3/4$ of the way through cooking for golden finish.

Chef Jim Camillo, Crystal Barn, Pittsford, NY

Flounder Rolled in Parmesan Crumbs

SERVES 4

8 flounder/sole fillets, (4–6 ounces each)
salt & pepper
2 tablespoons lemon juice
1 cup Ritz crackers, crushed into fine crumbs
3 tablespoons Parmesan cheese
2 tablespoons butter
fresh parsley, chopped

Preheat oven to 450°. Season flounder fillets with salt, pepper and lemon juice. Sprinkle with Ritz crumbs and Parmesan cheese. Roll fillets beginning at the tail (narrow end). Place in buttered casserole. Sprinkle with more crumbs and cheese. Dot with butter. Add 1–2 tablespoons of water to baking dish. Bake 10 minutes per inch of thickness of rolled fillet. Garnish with fresh parsley.

Sautéed Fillet of Sole with Grapes

SERVES 4

4 sole/flounder fillets, (6–8 ounces each)
salt & pepper
flour
$1/2$ cup vegetable oil
$1/4$ cup butter
$1/4$ pound whole green grapes
$1/4$ pound whole red grapes
$1/2$ cup white wine
1 tablespoon chopped red cherries
orange and lemon twists for garnish

Season fillets with salt and pepper; dip into flour, shaking off excess. Heat oil and butter in sauté pan. Sauté fillets, 2 minutes per side. Sauté green and red grapes in butter until soft to the touch. Add white wine and bring mixture to boil. Stir in chopped red cherries and pour sauce mixture over fillets. Serve hot, garnished with orange and lemon twists.

Flounder Florentine with Pine Nuts & Swiss Cheese

SERVES 12

5 pounds flounder/sole fillets (24 fillets)
$1/2$ pound Swiss cheese, shredded
2 eggs, slightly beaten
$1/2$ teaspoon white pepper
1 teaspoon salt
pinch of nutmeg
$1/2$ cup pine nuts, toasted
2 pounds frozen, chopped spinach, thawed and drained
3 tablespoons melted butter
paprika

Preheat oven to 450°. Mix cheese, eggs, spices and pine nuts into spinach. Lay out 12 fillets in baking pans. Place spinach filling along center of each fillet. Cover each spinach-topped fillet with second fillet, splitting the top fillet to show the filling. Brush with melted butter, sprinkle with paprika. Bake for approximately 15 minutes.

Flounders are a funny fish that start with one eye on each side of its head. One eye migrates, however, as the fish matures. If the eye migrates to the left, it is known as a "left-eyed flounder" if to the right, a "right-eyed flounder".

Flounder Sautéed with Brown Butter & Capers

SERVES 4

$1^1/_2$ pounds flounder/sole fillets
salt & pepper
flour for dusting
4 tablespoons canola oil
$^1/_3$ cup butter
2 tablespoons lemon juice
3 tablespoons capers, rinsed
1 tablespoon chopped parsley

Preheat 2 large skillets. Season the flounder and dredge in flour. Shake off excess. Add oil to pans. Brown fillets quickly on one side, turn over and finish on the other side. Transfer to plates. Add butter to one of the pans and brown. Quickly stir in the lemon juice, capers and parsley, swirl around and spoon over the fish.

Certified Master Chef Milos Cihelka, (ret)
Golden Mushroom, Southfield, MI

Baked Flounder Roll-Overs

SERVES 4

$1^1/_3$ pounds flounder/sole fillets
$1/_2$ cup chopped tomato
$1/_2$ cup chopped fresh mushrooms
$1/_4$ cup chopped scallions
1 can cream of mushroom soup
$1/_2$ cup white wine

Preheat oven to 350°. Combine tomatoes, mushrooms and scallions. Spread mixture over each fillet. Roll up fillets, secure with toothpicks and place in baking pan. Combine soup and wine in a small saucepan; stir and heat to simmer. Pour sauce over fish and bake for approximately 35 minutes or until cooked through.

Mom and I argued about including this recipe as I feared it too basic. She argued successfully that people like simple recipes requiring few ingredients and easy preparations with delicious results. Once again, Mom was right!

141

Sole Stuffed with Crabmeat

The original Joe Muer's was an institution in Detroit. Of all their seafood offerings, this sole recipe was a signature item for them. The restaurant has since relocated to Southfield, Michigan and is still serving their signature stuffed sole.

SERVES 6

10 large sole/flounder fillets, 6–8 ounces each

3 tablespoons melted butter

paprika

Crabmeat Stuffing

1 pound Jonah crabmeat

$1/2$ cup diced hard-boiled eggs

$1/2$ cup sautéed diced white onions

$1/2$ cup apple cider vinegar

2 tablespoons dry mustard

4 tablespoons Worcestershire sauce

$2/3$ cup mayonnaise

1 cup breadcrumbs

Preheat oven to 450°. Place flounder fillets on flat surface. Combine Crabmeat Stuffing ingredients and place $1/4$ cup of stuffing on the center of each fillet. Roll fillet around stuffing; place seam side down in a baking dish. Lightly brush with melted butter. Lightly dust with paprika. Bake for 8–10 minutes.

Geoffrey Browning, Joe Muer's Grill, Southfield, MI

Sole Sauté à la Peche

SERVES 2

$3/4$ to 1 pound sole/flounder fillets
salt & pepper
flour
$1/2$ cup vegetable oil
$1/4$ cup clarified butter

Sauce Veronique
1 tablespoon butter
1 tablespoon lemon juice
1 tablespoon curaçao
1 tablespoon peach brandy
$1/2$ cup sliced peaches

SOLE: Season fillets lightly with salt and pepper. Dredge lightly in flour. Preheat oil and clarified butter in sauté pan. Sauté fillets approximately $1^1/2$ minutes on each side, remove to hot platter.

SAUCE VERONIQUE: Melt butter and cook until light brown. Add lemon juice, curaçao and brandy. Heat mixture to boiling, stirring constantly. Add peaches and heat through. Pour over fillets and serve.

MONKFISH

Monkfish, also called goosefish or anglerfish, is a terrific eating fish despite its fearsome appearance. It's mild flavor and meaty firmness make it ideal for a variety of preparation styles, including soups and stews. Ask your fishmonger to trim your monkfish fillets if the outer membrane has not been removed.

Sherried Monkfish

SERVES 4

2 pounds monkfish fillets
salt & pepper
$1/4$ cup lemon juice
paprika
flour for dredging
3 tablespoons butter
$1/2$ cup sherry

Preheat oven to 350°. Cut monkfish fillet into quarters by cutting in half lengthwise and then cutting each half across so that each portion resembles a lobster tail. Season lightly with salt and pepper and sprinkle with lemon juice. Dredge seasoned fillet in a small amount of paprika then in flour. Shake off excess.

Sauté fillets slowly in hot butter for approximately 5 minutes. Sprinkle fillets with sherry. Simmer for 1 additional minute.

Remove fish from pan and place in casserole. Pour wine and butter from pan over top. Bake for about 10 minutes.

Monkfish with Oyster Mushrooms, Sugar Snap Peas, Capers & Brown Butter

SERVES 4

1 pound monkfish fillet, cut into 2-inch strips
salt & pepper to taste
3 tablespoons soft butter
3 ounces oyster mushrooms
1 tablespoon canola oil
1 cup blanched sugar snap peas (or fresh
**   snow pea pods)**
1 teaspoon capers
2 teaspoons lemon juice

Season monkfish with salt and pepper. Melt 1 tablespoon butter in hot pan. Cook butter until brown with a nutty aroma. Add monkfish and sauté 2–3 minutes. Remove from pan and keep warm. Reserve brown butter.

Salt and pepper oyster mushrooms. In a separate pan, lightly sauté seasoned oyster mushrooms in canola oil. When soft, add blanched snap peas and capers and heat through.

Meanwhile, add 1 tablespoon lemon juice to the brown butter pan and swirl. Pour over monkfish. Spoon mushroom/pea/caper mixture over monkfish and serve hot.

John Bubula, Marche, Chicago, IL

145

Monkfish Parmesan

SERVES 2

1 monkfish fillet (about 12 ounces)
1 tablespoon Dijon mustard
$1/2$ cup milk
1 egg
1 cup Ritz cracker crumbs
$1/4$ cup grated Parmesan cheese
flour for dusting
$1/4$ cup vegetable oil
4 tablespoons butter
1 tablespoon lemon juice
parsley, for garnish
lemon wedges, for garnish

Cut monkfish into thin slices (approximately 8 slices to 1 medium-sized fillet). Paint fillets with a light coating of mustard. Combine milk and egg. In a separate dish, combine Ritz cracker crumbs and Parmesan cheese. Dust fish with flour, shaking off excess. Dip into egg/milk mixture then dredge in cracker crumbs. Heat oil in sauté pan, add monkfish and cook until golden brown, 3–4 minutes per side.

Remove from pan to warm serving dish. Melt butter until bubbly; add lemon juice. Pour over monkfish and serve garnished with parsley and lemon wedges.

Pan-Roasted Monkfish with Sherry Ginger Broth

SERVES 2

2 monkfish fillets (6 ounces each)
salt and white pepper to taste
flour for dredging
1 tablespoon olive oil
$1/2$ teaspoon minced ginger root
4 shiitake mushrooms, stemmed and sliced
$1/4$ cup dry sherry
8–10 tablespoons chicken stock
6–8 dried bing cherries
1 small handful spinach, cleaned

Preheat oven to 450°.

MONKFISH: Heat sauté pan over high heat. Season fish with salt & pepper. Dredge in flour, shaking off excess. Add oil to pan, sear fish on both sides to golden brown. Remove fish to oven and cook until done, about 5-8 minutes.

SHERRY GINGER BROTH: Drain monkfish pan of excess oil and return to heat. Add ginger and shiitakes; cook 15–30 seconds. Deglaze pan with sherry, reducing by $2/3$. Add stock, cherries and spinach; cook until spinach is just wilted.

TO SERVE: Season broth to taste with salt and pepper and divide between 2 bowls. Keep warm. Add fish to bowls and serve.

Jay's Seafood Restaurant, Dayton, OH

147

San Diego Beer-Battered Fish Tacos with Baja Sauce

SERVES 4-6

1 pound monkfish fillet, cut into 1-inch pieces
1 12-ounce bottle Mexican beer
1 tablespoon Mexican seasoning
vegetable oil
1 cup flour
1 teaspoon salt
1 teaspoon sugar
$1/2$ teaspoon baking powder
1 cup Mexican beer
$1/2$ teaspoon hot sauce
12 fresh corn tortillas
1 lime, cut into wedges
1 cup shredded Monterey jack cheese
3 cups shredded green cabbage
$1/2$ red onion, cut into strips

Baja Sauce

$1/2$ cup sour cream
$1/2$ cup mayonnaise
2 teaspoons Mexican seasoning
1 small jalapeño pepper, seeded and diced
$1/4$ cup fresh lime juice
$1/2$ cup chopped fresh cilantro

MARINADE: Place fish in a large heavy-duty zip-top plastic bag. Combine 12 ounces beer and Mexican seasoning in a bowl, stirring well. Pour beer mixture over fish; seal bag. Chill 2–3 hours.

BAJA SAUCE: Combine all ingredients; stir well.

TO PREPARE: Pour oil to depth of 2 inches into a deep skillet or Dutch oven; heat to 350°. Combine flour and next 3 ingredients in a medium bowl. Whisk in 1 cup beer and hot sauce. Drain fish, discarding marinade. Coat fish in batter.

Cook fish in batches about 4 minutes or until done. Drain on paper towels.

TO SERVE: Place 2-3 pieces of fish on each tortilla. Squeeze lime wedges over fish; top with cheese, cabbage, onion and Baja sauce. Serve immediately.

OCEAN CATFISH

*Ocean catfish, also known as wolffish or loup de mer, are a
wonderful-tasting fish harvested from the Gulf of Maine.
Ocean catfish are not to be confused with fresh water catfish,
which don't compare in flavor or texture. "You are what you eat"
applies to ocean catfish — they are known to dine on a rich diet
of shellfish. It is this diet, fit for a king, that makes their meat
incredibly sweet and firm.*

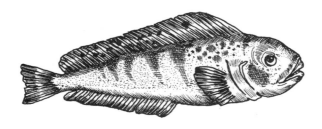

Ocean Catfish with Mushrooms

SERVES 4

**1 pound ocean catfish fillets
salt & pepper to taste
2 tablespoons vegetable oil
$1^1/_2$ tablespoons butter
$^1/_2$ lemon
$^1/_2$ pound mushrooms, thinly sliced
1 tablespoon chopped parsley**

Cut ocean catfish into 4 portions and season with salt and
pepper. Flour portions lightly. Preheat sauté pan. Add oil and
$^1/_2$ tablespoon butter. Add ocean catfish and sauté for 4–5
minutes each side. Remove fish to a hot plate. Squeeze $^1/_2$
lemon on top of it. Wipe pan clean. Add 1 tablespoon of butter
to pan. Add mushrooms and parsley and sauté for 2–3 minutes. Season to taste. Pour mushroom sauce on top of fish and
serve hot.

Poached Ocean Catfish with Creamy Tomato Sauce

SERVES 4

1 pound ocean catfish fillets
2 tomatoes
salt & pepper
$1/2$ cup water
$1/2$ cup white wine
1 teaspoon finely chopped scallion
1 teaspoon chopped fresh dill
1 tablespoon butter
$1/2$ pint heavy cream
dash cayenne pepper

Peel, seed and chop tomatoes. Season fish with salt and pepper. Place chopped tomatoes around fish; add water and wine, cover pan and bring to a fast boil. Turn heat down to simmer for 10 to 12 minutes. Remove fish and place it on a warm plate.

Add scallions, dill and butter to sauce. Bring remaining sauce to a fast boil and reduce until most of it evaporates. Add $1/2$ pint heavy cream. Bring to fast boil, add a dash of cayenne pepper and salt to taste. Pour tomato sauce over fish and serve.

Ocean Catfish Florentine

SERVES 4

1 pound ocean catfish fillets
1 pound frozen chopped spinach
2 tablespoons + 2 teaspoons butter
salt & pepper
1 pinch nutmeg
1 tablespoon flour
$1^1/_2$ cups light cream or milk
1 cup water
1 stem of parsley
1 teaspoon grated Parmesan cheese
1 teaspoon grated Romano cheese

Preheat oven to broil.

SPINACH: Cook spinach according to package instructions and drain. Heat 1 tablespoon butter in a sauté pan. Add spinach, salt and pepper and a pinch of nutmeg. Sauté for 5 minutes. Keep warm.

BÉCHAMEL SAUCE: Melt 1 tablespoon butter in sauté pan, gradually whisk in flour. Cook for 1-2 minutes over high heat. Add light cream and bring back to a simmer. Add salt and pepper and continue to cook until a creamy consistency is reached. Put aside and add 1 teaspoon butter to the top.

OCEAN CATFISH: Add 1 cup of water to a pan large enough to fit the ocean catfish fillets. Add 1 teaspoon butter to pan then top with ocean catfish fillets. Add parsley. Cover and simmer, for 5-6 minutes.

TO SERVE: Place spinach on ovenproof plate, top with fish, cover with Béchamel Sauce. Sprinkle with Parmesan and Romano cheese. Place the dish under the broiler until the cheese is melted and cream bubbles. Serve hot.

Broiled Ocean Catfish Nantaise

SERVES 4

1 pound ocean catfish fillets, cut into 4 portions
3 large shallots, finely chopped
salt & pepper to taste
vegetable oil as needed
1 cup white wine
1 egg yoke
2 tablespoons butter, cut into small pieces
1 tablespoon heavy cream

Preheat oven to broil. Bring shallots and wine to boil then reduce to slow simmer, cooking until wine is reduced to a couple tablespoons. Put aside to cool.

Season ocean catfish with salt and pepper. Place them in a lightly oiled baking pan; brush fish with oil and broil for 7–8 minutes. While fish is cooking, mix shallot/wine reduction with egg yoke in a heat-resistant bowl. Place bowl on a burner, at very low heat, and beat the mixture while adding butter and heavy cream. Keep beating over the burner until butter is melted.

Pour half of the sauce on a serving dish. Place fish on top of sauce, cover with remaining sauce, and serve hot.

Ocean Catfish Enchiladas

SERVES 8

2 pounds ocean catfish fillets, cut into 1-inch strips
olive oil
2 cups sour cream
7-ounce can diced green chilies
4 large scallions, chopped
$1/2$ cup chopped cilantro, plus additional for garnish
$1^{1}/2$ teaspoons ground cumin
salt & pepper
24-ounce jar of mild salsa
1 yellow pepper, finely chopped
1 red pepper, finely chopped
2 cups grated sharp cheddar cheese
8 – 8-inch diameter flour tortillas

Preheat oven to 350°. Sauté ocean catfish in olive oil for approximately 2–3 minutes, until just browned.

Butter a 13x9 glass dish. Mix $1^{3}/4$ cup sour cream, chilies, scallions, cilantro and cumin in large bowl. Mix in ocean catfish and 1 cup cheddar cheese. Season with salt and pepper.

Spoon $1/2$ cup mixture down the center of each tortilla. Roll up tortilla and arrange seam side down in baking dish. Pour salsa over enchiladas. Sprinkle peppers over top.

Cover and bake for approximately 45 minutes. Uncover, sprinkle with 1 cup cheddar cheese and bake for 5 additional minutes, until cheese melts. Top with remaining sour cream and garnish with cilantro.

RED SNAPPER

Genuine American red snapper is caught in the warm waters off the coast of Florida in the Gulf of Mexico. It is a highly regulated species with limited availability. Because of this, much of the snapper sold in the United States is imported from foreign markets. Imported snappers may be substituted in these recipes.

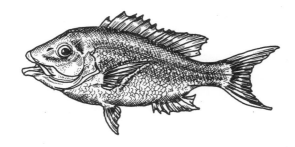

Zesty Snapper

SERVES 4

$1^1/_2$ pounds red snapper fillets
6 slices bacon, chopped
$3/_4$ cup onion, thinly sliced
dash of garlic salt
1 cup pitted black olives, coarsely chopped
pepper to taste
$1/_2$ cup soft breadcrumbs
1 tablespoon lemon juice
2 tablespoons chopped parsley

Preheat oven to 450°. Fry bacon over medium heat until crisp. Drain fat, reserving 1 tablespoon. Sauté sliced onions in bacon fat until soft and translucent. Place fish fillets in single layer in well-greased baking dish. Combine bacon, onion and remaining ingredients; spoon over fish fillets. Bake for 10–15 minutes until fish flakes easily with a fork.

Red Snapper with Sweet Potato Cakes & Mojito Sauce

SERVES 6

6 red snapper fillets
2 tablespoons olive oil
salt and pepper

Sweet Potato Cakes

3 sweet potatoes, baked, cooled and scooped
    from their skins
$1/2$ medium-sized onion, chopped
$1^1/2$ teaspoons minced garlic clove
$1^1/2$ teaspoons minced jalapeño chili
1 tablespoon olive oil
$3/4$ cup panko (Japanese breadcrumbs)
$1/2$ cup cornmeal
2 tablespoons olive oil

Mojito Sauce

1 cup olive oil
2 tablespoons garlic, minced
$3/4$ cup orange juice
$1/4$ cup lime juice
2 tablespoons fresh cilantro

SWEET POTATO CAKES: Heat oil in sauté pan and add onion, garlic and jalapeno. Saute until golden brown, then cool. Combine scooped sweet potato, sauté vegetables and breadcrumbs. Mix together and form into 2-ounce cakes. Dust with cornmeal on both sides. Pan fry for one minute per side in non-stick sauté pan.

MOJITO SAUCE: Combine all ingredients in a blender and blend well.

RED SNAPPER: Preheat grill. Brush snapper with olive oil and season with salt and pepper. Grill for approximately 5 minutes per side.

TO SERVE: Drizzle plate with Mojito Sauce. Top with sweet potato cakes then add grilled snapper. Drizzle additional Mojito Sauce over all then serve.

Chef Paul Weber, Foley Fish House,
Renaissance Hotel, Times Square, New York, NY

Pan-Fried Snapper in Garlic Butter

SERVES 4

$1^1/_2$ pounds red snapper fillets
salt & pepper
4 tablespoons milk
$1/_4$ cup flour
$1/_3$ cup vegetable oil
6 tablespoons butter
1 tablespoon chopped garlic
lemon juice
parsley for garnish

Lightly season snapper fillets with salt and pepper. Dip fillets in milk and dredge in flour. Shake off excess flour. Heat oil in large sauté pan, add snapper and cook for 2–3 minutes. Turn and sauté for 2–3 minutes more. Transfer fish to a warm serving platter.

Wipe sauté pan clean. Melt butter over medium-high heat, add garlic, and sauté to heat through. Sprinkle fillets with lemon juice. Pour garlic butter over fillets. Garnish with lemon slices and parsley.

Grilled Red Snapper with Corn Salsa

SERVES 6

6 portions red snapper (8 ounces each)
salt & pepper
vegetable oil
breadcrumbs

Corn Salsa

kernels of 1 ear of corn
zest of $1/2$ lime, finely grated
1 ripe avocado, mashed
juice of 2 limes
1 cup seeded and diced tomatoes
1 tablespoon olive oil
1 tablespoon chopped cilantro leaves
$1/2$ teaspoon mashed garlic
Tabasco

CORN SALSA: Mix salsa ingredients together and refrigerate for 2 hours. Allow to return to room temperature before serving.

SNAPPER: Preheat a grill or heavy skillet. Season fish with salt and pepper, brush with oil, sprinkle lightly with breadcrumbs. Oil grill and place fish over medium heat. Grill fish approximately 5 minutes per side depending on thickness.

Serve bordered with Corn Salsa.

FINNAN HADDIE

Finnan haddie is smoked cod or smoked haddock. Finnan haddie is usually sold in the fillet form and features a rich golden hue. It is important to get 100 percent natural finnan haddie as chemicals interfere with the genuine smoky flavor. We love finnan haddie during the holiday season.

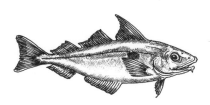

Creamed Finnan Haddie

1 pound finnan haddie fillets
1 cup milk
$1/2$ cup heavy cream
$1/4$ cup flour
$1/4$ cup butter
$1/2$ small package Velveeta® cheese
1 teaspoon prepared mustard
$1/2$ teaspoon Worcestershire sauce
paprika

Preheat oven to 450°. Heat milk and cream. Make paste of flour and butter. When milk is hot, add flour mixture. Cut Velveeta cheese up into small pieces and add to mixture. Add mustard and Worcestershire sauce. Stir all ingredients until they dissolve. Cook until it comes to a boil, stirring to prevent burning.

Cut smoked haddock fillets into large pieces, put into a pan and cover with boiling water. Allow to simmer about 15 minutes. Remove fish from water and add to cream sauce.

Pour all ingredients into a casserole dish. Sprinkle with paprika, dot with butter and bake for 10–12 minutes.

Baked Finnan Haddie au Gratin

SERVES 2

2 portions of finnan haddie (6 ounces each)
Cream Sauce
6 tablespoons butter
6 tablespoons flour
$1/2$ cup clam juice
$1/2$ cup light cream
1 cup milk
Casserole
Dash of Worcestershire sauce
1 cup grated sharp cheddar cheese
3 tablespoons butter
Ritz cracker crumbs for topping

CREAM SAUCE: Melt butter, whisk in flour. Cook for approximately $1/2$ minute. Do not allow to brown. Whisk in remaining liquids gradually until combined. Cook until creamy consistency.

FINNAN HADDIE: Preheat oven to 400°. Butter a large casserole dish. Place finnan haddie in casserole with a touch of water and bake for 10–15 minutes, depending on thickness. Mix half of grated cheese with Cream Sauce. Add Worcestershire sauce. Bring to a boil. Coat fish portions with Cream Sauce and sprinkle with other half of grated cheese and Ritz cracker crumbs. Dot with butter and bake until golden brown, approximately 25 minutes.

Quiche Ecossaise

SERVES 4–6

$1/2$ pound finnan haddie fillets
1 quart milk
9-inch pie plate lined with unbaked pie crust
$1/4$ pound smoked ham, cut into small dice
$1/4$ pound bacon, cut into small dice
1/4 pound grated Swiss cheese
3 eggs
$1/2$ pint of light cream
salt & pepper
nutmeg

Preheat oven to 350°.

FINNAN HADDIE: Soak finnan haddie in 1 quart of milk for 1 hour then bake in milk for 1 hour. Drain milk. Break up finnan haddie into large flakes.

QUICHE: Partially bake pie crust for 7 minutes. Sauté ham and bacon until fat is removed. Lay half the Swiss cheese on bottom of pie shell. Sprinkle half of bacon mixture on top of cheese. Spread finnan haddie over pie and add remaining bacon. Finish with remaining cheese.

CUSTARD: Mix 3 eggs with $1/2$ pint of light cream and beat well, about 3 minutes. Season with salt and pepper. Pour slowly into pie shell until it reaches top of crust. Sprinkle with nutmeg.

Bake quiche on a cookie sheet for approximately 25–30 minutes. Quiche is done when knife inserted in center comes out clean.

TUNA

Tuna has come a long way from its days of "canned only" albacore. Restaurants across America are featuring fresh yellowfin tuna. Yellowfin tuna is a hearty fish that even beef eaters will enjoy. We recommend preparing tuna medium-rare to optimize flavor and texture. Proper handling of tuna is essential—keep it cold and keep it covered. Marinating tuna should always be refrigerated.

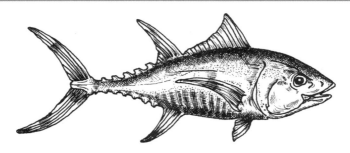

Grilled Sweet & Sour Tuna Steaks

SERVES 4

4 yellowfin tuna steaks (8 ounces each)
$1/2$ cup dry sherry
2 tablespoons grated ginger root
2 tablespoons light soy sauce
1 teaspoon light honey
1 teaspoon maple syrup
1 tablespoon minced garlic
2 teaspoons dark sesame oil
2 tablespoons minced cilantro (optional)

Preheat broiler or grill. Combine all ingredients and marinate tuna for 10 minutes. Remove steaks from marinade and broil or grill 5–8 minutes on each side, turning once and basting with marinade. Serve hot.

Certified Master Chef Michael Russell, Motor City Casino, Detroit, MI

162

Grilled Tuna with Gazpacho

SERVES 4

Gazpacho
> $1/4$ cup tomato paste
> 3 tablespoons wine vinegar
> $1/4$ cup clam juice
> $1/4$ cup olive oil
> pinch of ground cumin
> pinch of cayenne pepper
> 1 teaspoon mashed garlic

Vegetables
> $1/2$ cup peeled cucumber
> $1/2$ cup scallions
> $1/2$ cup chopped celery
> $1/2$ cup chopped green pepper
> $1/2$ cup chopped red pepper

Tuna
> 4 tuna steaks (8 ounces each)
> salt & fresh ground pepper
> 3 tablespoons vegetable oil
> 2 tablespoons breadcrumbs

Preheat grill.

GAZPACHO: In a glass, ceramic or stainless steel bowl, mix all gazpacho ingredients together. Scrape seeds from cucumber and cut into $1/4$-inch thick, 2-inch long sticks. Cut scallions on the bias into 2-inch pieces, using white and light green part only. Stir all vegetables into gazpacho.

TUNA: Season tuna with salt and pepper, oil both sides and sprinkle lightly with breadcrumbs. Place on a hot grill and sear quickly on one side, turn and finish on the other side. Cook medium-rare. Transfer to plates; spoon gazpacho over fish.

Certified Master Chef Milos Cihelka (ret),
Golden Mushroom, Southfield, MI

163

Char-Broiled Yellowfin Tuna with Mustard Caper Butter

SERVES 4

4 portions yellowfin tuna (8 ounces each)
1 tablespoon country style Dijon mustard
1 tablespoon capers
pinch white pepper
$1/4$ pound butter, softened
mayonnaise

Preheat broiler. Blend mustard, capers and pepper into butter. Paint tuna with mayonnaise. Broil tuna for approximately 5–7 minutes. Remove tuna from broiler and top with mustard combination. Return tuna to broiler until topping is bubbly, about 1–2 minutes. Serve immediately.

Adams Rib, Zionsville, IN

Sesame Pan-Seared Yellowfin Tuna

SERVES 4

1 pound yellowfin tuna steaks
salt & pepper to taste
sesame seeds
vegetable or olive oil
chopped chives
soy sauce

Cut tuna into 2-inch logs. Season tuna with salt and pepper, then roll in sesame seeds, pressing to coat. Heat oil in large sauté pan. When oil is very hot, sear each tuna "log" for 1 minute on all sides. Carefully slice tuna into $1/4$-inch slices.

Arrange on plate and garnish with chopped chives. Serve with soy sauce.

Peppercorn Tuna (Tuna au Poivre)

SERVES 2

2 tuna steaks (8 ounces each, about 1-inch thick)
salt
1 tablespoon +1 teaspoon coarsely ground pepper
$1^1/_2$ tablespoons butter
$1/_4$ cup vegetable oil
juice of $1/_2$ lemon
1 scallion, chopped
$1/_2$ cup white wine
$1/_2$ cup heavy cream

Season tuna with salt and pepper. Sauté tuna in a pan with $1/_2$ tablespoon butter and vegetable oil for 5 minutes per side. Place tuna on a hot plate and pour lemon juice on top.

Wipe pan clean. Add 1 tablespoon butter and scallions. Sweat scallions for 2–3 minutes. Add wine and bring to a fast boil. When wine is almost evaporated, add heavy cream, bring to a fast boil and reduce. Pour sauce over tuna and serve.

Tuna Provençale

SERVES 2

2 tuna steaks (8 ounces each, about 1-inch thick)
$1/4$ cup olive oil
1 small onion, sliced
4 tomatoes, seeded and cut in chunks
2 teaspoons parsley
1 tablespoon chopped black olives (optional)
pinch thyme
pinch oregano
2 teaspoons capers
2 cloves garlic, finely chopped
$1/2$ cup white wine or water
salt & pepper to taste

Preheat oven to 350°.

Sauté tuna steaks in oil until brown, using oven-proof pan. Add sliced onions, chopped tomatoes, parsley, black olives, thyme, oregano, capers, garlic and white wine and cook 5 minutes. Season to taste.

Place pan in oven and bake for 20 minutes. Transfer tuna to warmed serving plate. Top with sauce and serve.

Grilled Tuna with Rainforest Glaze

SERVES 6

6 tuna steaks (6 ounces each)
1 tablespoon cornstarch
1 tablespoon water
1 cup thinly sliced scallions

Rainforest Glaze

1 cup pineapple juice
$1/2$ teaspoon grated lemon rind
1 cup cranberry juice cocktail
$1/2$ teaspoon grated orange rind
1 cup apricot nectar
$1/2$ teaspoon salt
1 tablespoon sugar
1 tablespoon lime juice
2 tablespoon grated peeled fresh ginger
2 teaspoons seeded and chopped jalapeño peppers

RAINFOREST GLAZE: Combine glaze ingredients in a large saucepan. Bring to a boil and cook until reduced to $1^{1}/2$ cups, about 15 minutes. Remove from heat. Combine cornstarch and water in a small bowl, stir well with a whisk then add this mixture to above pan. Bring to a boil; cook 1 minute, stirring constantly. Remove from heat; stir in scallions.

TUNA: Preheat grill to medium-high heat. Place tuna on grill rack coated with cooking spray, grill 3 minutes on each side or until medium-rare or desired degree of doneness. Baste frequently with glaze. Remove tuna from grill, plate, drizzle with Rainforest Glaze and serve immediately.

Robert's Food Store, North Madison, CT

Balsamic Glazed Tuna

SERVES 4

4 tuna steaks (6 ounces each)
$1^1/_4$ teaspoons coarsely ground black pepper
$1/_4$ teaspoon salt
$1/_4$ cup chicken broth
1 tablespoon balsamic vinegar
4 teaspoons dark brown sugar
1 tablespoon low-sodium soy sauce
$1/_2$ teaspoon cornstarch
$1/_4$ cup chopped scallions

Coat a grill or sauté pan with cooking spray. Preheat pan over medium-high heat. Season tuna with salt and pepper. Place fish in pan, cook 3 minutes on each side until medium-rare or desired doneness. Remove from heat.

Combine broth, vinegar, sugar, soy sauce, and cornstarch in small saucepan. Bring to a boil; cook 1 minute, stirring constantly.

TO SERVE: Spoon glaze over fish; top with scallions.

Robert's Food Store, North Madison, CT

Broiled Tuna Teriyaki

SERVES 4

$1^1/_3$ pounds tuna steaks
1 tablespoon peeled, finely chopped ginger
$1/_4$ cup soy sauce
2 tablespoons oil
1 tablespoon honey

Preheat broiler or grill. Combine all ingredients except fish. Pour marinade over tuna and marinate, refrigerated, for half an hour. Broil or grill tuna 4–6 inches from heat source, brushing with marinade, approximately 4 minutes per side, just until cooked throughout.

Foley Fish has a tradition of providing weekly "take home" fish for our employees. Our founder, M.F. introduced the practice as he believed that the employees would take extra care with the fish "down the line" if they thought the fish they were handling might end up on their kitchen table. In the summertime fresh tuna for the grill is a favorite "take home" fish!

Pancetta-Wrapped Tuna with Chanterelles

SERVES 10

2 tuna loins, cut like a roast, each about 6 inches
  long, $1^1/_2$ inches thick and $1^1/_2$ inches wide
  ($1^1/_4$ pounds per loin)
1 pound pancetta, thinly sliced
salt and freshly ground white pepper
butcher's twine for wrapping tuna
6 tablespoons unsalted butter

Chanterelles

10 ounces chanterelles, quartered if large
2 tablespoons finely chopped shallots
salt & white pepper
$1/_2$ cup sherry vinegar
$1/_2$ cup dry white wine
$1/_2$ cup low-sodium chicken broth
4 tablespoons chopped chives

TUNA: Spread a piece of plastic wrap on counter. Lay out half
of pancetta slices vertically, each slice slightly overlapping its
neighboring slice. Season tuna very lightly with salt and
pepper and place it crosswise in the center of the pancetta.
One by one, wrap each piece of pancetta around the tuna,
pressing the pancetta gently against the tuna and keeping the
rows even. Secure the pancetta by tying the tuna at 1–inch
intervals with kitchen twine, just as you would a meat roast.
Wrap tuna in the plastic wrap and refrigerate. Repeat for
second tuna loin.

TO PREPARE: Preheat oven to 450°. Melt 1 tablespoon butter
each in 2 large ovenproof sauté pans over medium heat. When
hot, add a tuna loin and sear tuna for 2 minutes on each of its
4 sides, then slide pan into the oven for 5 minutes. After 5 minutes in the oven the tuna will be rare, cooked on the outside
and warm but not colored anywhere else. If this is too rare,
add 1–2 minutes to baking time. Lift tuna out of pan and onto

a warm platter, cover loosely with foil. Reserve half the fat from one of the pans.

CHANTERELLES: Return pan to stovetop and turn heat to medium-low and toss in chanterelles. Cover pan and cook mushrooms until almost tender but not colored, about 3-5 minutes. Add shallots, season with salt and pepper and cook another minute or so to soften shallots. Pour in vinegar and reduce it by 3/4. Add white wine, bring it to a boil and allow it to cook away before adding the chicken stock. Add stock, reduce it by half, then remove pan from heat and swirl in remaining 4 tablespoons butter, one small piece at a time. Sprinkle in chives.

TO SERVE: Cut tuna into 20 slices using a long, thin, very sharp knife, removing kitchen twine as you slice. Serve 2 slices per plate and surround with chanterelles and sauce. Good served atop mashed potatoes.

Tuna with Spinach & Balsamic Caper Sauce

SERVES 4

4 tuna steaks (6 ounces each, about $3/4$-inch thick)
$1/4$ cup dry breadcrumbs
1 tablespoon pesto sauce
1 tablespoon water
cooking spray
$1/4$ cup balsamic vinegar
1 tablespoon capers
$1/4$ cup diced shallots
6 cups fresh stemmed and torn spinach (1 pound)
$1/2$ cup dry white wine
$1/4$ teaspoon freshly ground black pepper

Combine breadcrumbs, pesto, and water in a small bowl, tossing well. Pat breadcrumb mixture on both sides of each tuna steak.

Heat a large non-stick skillet coated with cooking spray over medium-high heat. Add tuna and cook 2 minutes on each side or until medium-rare or desired degree of doneness. Remove tuna from pan and keep warm. Stir in vinegar and capers, scraping pan to loosen browned bits and cook 1 minute.

Heat a large Dutch oven coated with cooking spray over medium-high heat until hot. Add shallots and sauté 3 minutes or until tender. Add spinach and sauté 1 minute. Add wine and pepper; partially cover and cook for 2 minutes or until the spinach wilts. Remove spinach to warm platter.

To Serve: Place tuna over spinach; drizzle with Balsamic Caper Sauce.

SALMON

*Salmon is a wonderfully rich, firm fish featuring a beautiful
orange to red hue. Salmon is considered a "heart-healthy" fish
because of its naturally occurring omega 3 oils. Most salmon today
is farm-raised, though there are certain seasons for
wild salmon from the West Coast. Either wild or farm-raised
salmon can be used in these recipes.*

Tangy Grilled Salmon Steaks

SERVES 4

4 salmon steaks, 1-inch thick
vegetable oil
$1/3$ cup apricot jam
2 teaspoons horseradish
$1^1/2$ teaspoons cider vinegar

Marinate steaks in vegetable oil for 15–30 minutes. Preheat
grill. Combine jam, horseradish and vinegar. Drain steaks and
baste with apricot mixture. Grill steaks 5 minutes on each
side, basting frequently with sauce.

Martini Salmon

SERVES 6

4 salmon fillets (6 ounces each, about $1/3$-inch thick)
7 tablespoons butter, divided
salt & pepper
$1/2$ cup dry vermouth
2 tablespoons chopped shallots
zest of lemon, finely grated
1 tablespoon lemon juice
1 tablespoon Dijon mustard
2 tablespoons chopped capers
3 tablespoons chopped parsley

Preheat 2 large non-stick skillets. Add 2 tablespoons butter to each pan. Place the fillets in pans without overlapping. Sprinkle fillets lightly with salt and pepper, cover pans and cook over medium-high heat 4–6 minutes per side. Using a large spatula, transfer them to warm plates.

Pour vermouth into skillets and bring to a boil. Consolidate contents of pans into 1 pan. Whip in the remaining 3 tablespoons butter and remaining ingredients; spoon over fish.

Poached Salmon Steaks

SERVES 4

4 salmon steaks (1-inch thick)
1 quart water
$1/2$ cup white wine
10 peppercorns
2 bay leaves
1 tablespoon salt

Combine water, wine, peppercorns, bay leaves and salt and bring to a boil. Place salmon steaks in boiling water and simmer 10 minutes. Remove from heat and allow salmon to cool in liquid. Remove steaks from pan. Carefully remove bones and skin. Serve immediately warm or refrigerate and serve chilled with your favorite vegetable and salad.

Salmon Steak Sandwich

SERVES 4

4 poached salmon steaks, boned and skinned
  (see recipe above)
2 tablespoons coarsely chopped fresh basil
$1/3$ cup mayonnaise
4 croissants or other sandwich rolls
16 thin slices cucumber

Combine basil and mayonnaise. Refrigerate 30 minutes for flavors to mingle. Spread mayonnaise and basil on lower half of croissant. Top with four cucumber slices and then salmon and other half of roll.

Baked Salmon with Dill

SERVES 4

$1^1/_3$ pounds fresh salmon fillets
2 tablespoons butter
1 teaspoon dried dill
freshly ground black pepper to taste

Preheat oven to 425°. Place salmon portions on large rectangular pieces of aluminum foil. Top each with butter pats and season with dill and pepper. Bring longer ends of foil together and double fold; fold in two remaining sides. All edges should be well sealed to trap steam while cooking. Place foil packets on a baking sheet and bake for 10 minutes.

This can also be done on the grill; be sure to use low heat, double the foil and heat until fish is cooked throughout.

Robert's Food Store, North Madison, CT

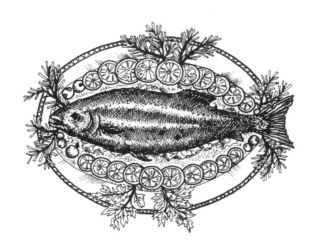

Toasted Coriander Atlantic Salmon

SERVES 4

4 salmon portions (8 ounces each)
2 tablespoons ground coriander seed
$1/4$ cup canola oil, divided
2 large eggplant, peeled and diced small
$1/4$ cup crushed garlic
1 yellow onion, minced
$1/2$ pound shiitake mushrooms
$1/2$ pound shaved fennel root
2 cups fish broth (see page 54) or clam juice
18-ounce can chopped tomatoes
fresh rosemary to taste
2 tablespoons honey
salt & pepper to taste

STEW: Heat heavy pan very hot then add 2 tablespoons of oil to pan; stir in eggplant quickly. Continue to stir until brown all over, then add garlic, onion, mushroom and fennel. Sauté for 10–12 minutes, until tender. Add fish stock, tomatoes and rosemary, then add honey and simmer for about 15–20 minutes. If stew gets too dry, add more stock. Season to taste. (May be prepared ahead).

SALMON: Brush 2 tablespoons canola oil on salmon then sprinkle coriander on top and bottom of fish. Pan sear the salmon or bake, whichever is desired.

TO SERVE: Place stew in bottom of large, wide bowl and place salmon on top. Garnish with fresh rosemary sprig.

J.S. Freedman, Sole Proprietor, Worcester, MA

177

White Wine & Spring Thyme Salmon

SERVES 6

> 2 pounds salmon fillets
> $1/2$ cup dry white wine or chicken broth
> 3 tablespoons olive oil
> 1 tablespoon thyme leaves
> 1 teaspoon ground mustard
> dash onion salt
> $1/2$ teaspoon ground white pepper
> $1/2$ teaspoon garlic salt

Combine white wine, olive oil, thyme, mustard, onion, pepper and garlic salt. Pour over salmon and cover. Refrigerate 30 minutes, turning occasionally. Preheat broiler or grill. Place fish on broiler pan or grill and spoon enough marinade over fish to cover top. Broil or grill to desired doneness, turning once.

Sesame-Encrusted Salmon

SERVES 10

> 5 pounds salmon fillets
> 2 cups sesame oil
> $2/3$ cup soy sauce
> $2/3$ cup rice wine vinegar
> $1/8$ cup minced garlic
> $1/8$ cup minced ginger
> 5 ounces white sesame seeds

Combine sesame oil, soy sauce, rice wine vinegar, garlic and ginger in a bowl and marinate salmon, refrigerated, for 24 hours. Preheat oven to 450°. Press sesame seeds into skinless side of fillet. Sear seeded side of salmon in a hot sauté pan. Turn onto a cookie sheet and bake for 5 minutes.

Graul's Market, Ruxton, MD

178

Grilled Orange-Bourbon Salmon

SERVES 4

4 salmon fillets, skinned, (6 ounces each, 1-inch thick)

Orange-Bourbon Marinade

$1/4$ **cup bourbon**
$1/4$ **cup orange juice**
$1/4$ **cup low-sodium soy sauce**
$1/4$ **cup packed brown sugar**
$1/4$ **cup chopped scallions**
3 tablespoons chopped fresh chives
2 tablespoons fresh lemon juice
2 garlic cloves chopped
cooking spray

Combine marinade ingredients in a large zip-top plastic bag. Add salmon to bag. Seal and marinate in refrigerator for $1\,1/2$ hours, turning bag occasionally. Preheat grill or broiler. Remove salmon from bag, discarding marinade. Place salmon on grill rack or broiler pan coated with cooking spray. Cook 6 minutes on each side or until fish flakes easily when tested with a fork.

Robert's Food Store, North Madison, CT

Salmon with Tarragon-Leek Sauce

SERVES 8

8 salmon fillets (6 ounces each)
1 stick butter
4 large leeks (white and pale green part only)
$1^1/_4$ cups dry vermouth
$1^1/_4$ cups whipping cream
$^1/_4$ cup chopped fresh parsley
2 tablespoons fresh tarragon, chopped
salt & pepper
flour
extra chopped parsley for garnish

SAUCE: Melt 4 tablespoons butter in large skillet over low heat. Sauté leeks in butter until soft and transparent, approximately 5 minutes. Add vermouth and boil on high until liquid is reduced to 2 tablespoons, about 5 minutes. Add cream and boil until thickened to sauce consistency. Stir in parsley and tarragon. Season with salt and pepper. Remove from heat, cover to keep warm.

SALMON: Sprinkle salmon with salt and pepper. Dust salmon lightly with flour. Melt 2 tablespoon butter in each of 2 large non-stick skillets over medium-high heat. Add 4 salmon fillets to each skillet and cook for 3 minutes per side.

TO SERVE: Transfer salmon to plates; spoon sauce over fillets. Garnish with parsley.

HALIBUT

Halibut is the largest fish in the flounder family. It is as sweet and mild as its smaller flounder cousins but has a thicker, firmer flake. Halibut is sourced from both the East and West coasts. The Western halibut fishery is regulated by government quotas, so this fish is only available fresh at certain times of the year. Both Eastern and Western halibut are interchangeable in recipes.

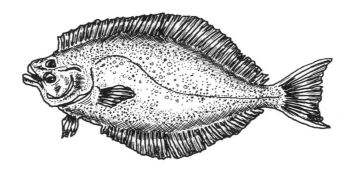

Barbecued Halibut

SERVES 6

2 pounds halibut fillets

Marinade

2 tablespoons frozen pineapple juice concentrate
$1/3$ cup hickory-smoked barbecue sauce
1 tablespoon lemon juice
3 tablespoons salad oil
1 tablespoon minced onion
$1/4$ teaspoon salt

Combine marinade ingredients. Marinate halibut, refrigerated, for 30 minutes. Grill over medium-high heat approximately 5 minutes on each side, basting occasionally with marinade during cooking.

181

Halibut with Herbed Breadcrumbs

SERVES 4

4 halibut fillets (8 ounces each)
1 teaspoon roasted garlic
$1/3$ cup mayonnaise
salt & pepper
flour
2 tablespoons olive oil
2 tablespoons melted butter

Herbed Breadcrumbs
8 slices fresh white bread
3 tablespoons butter
3 tablespoons chopped parsley
salt & pepper

HERBED BREADCRUMBS: Place bread in food processor and process into crumbs. Add butter until moist. Stir in parsley. Season with salt and pepper

HALIBUT: Preheat oven to 350°. Combine garlic with mayonnaise. Season fillets with salt and pepper. Dredge in flour. Preheat sauté pan. Add oil. Cook halibut for about 3 minutes, flip to second side. Top with garlic-mayonnaise mixture and then fresh breadcrumbs. Drizzle with melted butter. Bake for 6–7 minutes.

Serve atop a bed of sautéed leeks with mashed potatoes.

Ron L. Wise, Parkers Blue Ash Grill, Cincinnati, OH

Mushroom & Basil Halibut Bake

SERVES 4

1^1/$_3$ pounds halibut fillets
2 tablespoons olive oil
salt & pepper to taste
^{1}/$_4$ cup shredded basil leaves
^{1}/$_2$ pound mushrooms, sliced
^{1}/$_4$ cup white cooking wine

Preheat oven to 425°. Place fish in a lightly oiled baking pan. Drizzle remaining oil on top and season with salt and pepper. Sprinkle basil evenly over fish and top with mushrooms. Pour in wine and cover pan with foil. Bake about 10 minutes, until cooked through.

Serve with cooking juices spooned over halibut.

Robert's Food Store, North Madison, CT

Halibut can become quite scarce between December and March when Western halibut is off season and Eastern halibut are hard to come by owing to harsher winter fishing conditions in the Northeast. Plan your halibut meals for spring through autumn for the best pricing and availability.

183

Halibut with Cream Sauce

SERVES 4

1 pound halibut fillets, cut into 4 portions
2 shallots, chopped
1 tablespoon butter
$1/4$ cup white wine
$1/4$ cup water
salt
$1/2$ cup heavy cream
cayenne pepper

Preheat oven to 450°. Place chopped shallots and butter in a shallow baking dish. Add fish, then wine and water. Season with salt to taste. Cover with aluminum foil and bake for 10 minutes.

Remove fish and place in a hot serving dish. Keep warm. Reduce cooking liquid by half, add heavy cream and bring back to boil for about 3 minutes, stirring occasionally. Add cayenne pepper. Pour sauce over fish and serve.

Baked Tomato Halibut

SERVES 2

1 pound halibut fillet, cut into 2 portions
1 tomato, sliced into 6 pieces
1 onion, sliced into 6 pieces
1 lemon, sliced into 6 pieces
2 tablespoons butter
$1/2$ cup white wine
salt & pepper
2 tablespoons breadcrumbs
1 bunch parsley, chopped

Preheat oven to 450°. Place fish in a baking dish with wine and butter. Place sliced tomato, onion and lemon on and around the fish. Season with salt and pepper and bake, covered, for 10 minutes.

Remove fish from pan; place in hot serving dish. Keep warm. Place cooking liquid in saucepan and bring to boil. Add breadcrumbs and chopped parsley. Pour over fish and serve hot with steamed broccoli.

Potato-Crusted Halibut with Tomato Vinaigrette

SERVES 4

Tomato Vinaigrette

$1/4$ cup each: red and yellow tomatoes, diced and seeded

$1/4$ cup julienned Vidalia onions

2 tablespoons chopped fresh basil

2 tablespoons chopped fresh chives

$1/3$ cup malt vinegar

$1/2$ cup extra-virgin olive oil

salt & pepper to taste

Halibut

4 halibut fillets (6 ounces each)

salt, pepper and Old Bay seasoning to taste

2 cups instant potato flakes

2 tablespoons olive oil

Preheat oven to 450°. Combine vinaigrette ingredients. Refrigerate for 2 hours.

Season fish with salt, pepper and Old Bay. Dredge in potato flakes. Heat olive oil in a non-stick pan. Sauté each side until golden brown. Remove to oven and bake for 6–8 minutes.

Toss Tomato Vinaigrette with mixed greens and serve halibut atop greens.

Chef Darren Anklam, Windows, Renaissance, Baltimore, MD

SWORDFISH

*Swordfish are at their peak of flavor in the late summer and
early fall when they are swimming in New England waters.
These migratory fish winter in warm southern waters then swim
up from the Gulf of Mexico feasting on a rich diet of mackerel,
bluefish and shellfish. By the time they reach our waters, they are
big, beefy and full of flavor and moistness. Plan your summer
menus to include fresh, grilled swordfish.*

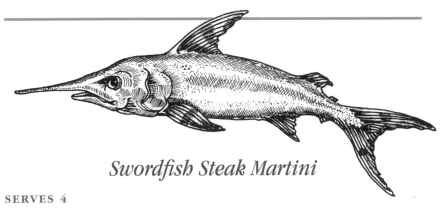

Swordfish Steak Martini

SERVES 4

**4 swordfish steaks (8 ounces each)
$1/2$ cup dry vermouth
$1/4$ cup gin
salt & fresh ground pepper
3 tablespoons melted butter
$1/4$ cup chopped green olives**

Marinate swordfish in vermouth and gin in covered glass dish, refrigerated, for 2 hours. Remove from marinade, pat dry with paper towel, reserve juice. Preheat 2 non-stick skillets; add butter and swordfish. Over medium-high heat cook steaks until you see their juice rising to the surface. Turn and finish on other side. Do not overcook.

Place cooked swordfish on plates. Swirl marinade in the skillets. Consolidate marinade into one pan, add olives, reduce if necessary by boiling, then spoon over fish.

187

Native Swordfish with Fresh Tomato Salsa & Yellow Tomato Coulis

While there are a few steps to this recipe, it is well worth the effort — the plate looks beautiful and the flavors shout summer! Plus, the tomato salsa and coulis can be made ahead.

SERVES 4

4 swordfish steaks (8 ounces each)
Yellow Tomato Coulis (see below)
Fresh Tomato Salsa (see below)
12 slices grilled squash (zucchini and summer squash)
salt & pepper
extra-virgin olive oil

Yellow Tomato Coulis

$1/4$ cup extra-virgin olive oil
$1/2$ Spanish onion, peeled and finely sliced
1 tablespoon minced garlic
$1/4$ cup fresh basil, sliced
4 yellow tomatoes, washed, cored and quartered
salt & pepper

Fresh Tomato Salsa

4 ripe red tomatoes, cored and sliced into 1-inch cubes
1 tablespoon minced garlic
$1/2$ Bermuda onion, peeled and finely sliced
$1/2$ cup extra-virgin olive oil
1 tablespoon each fresh mint, cilantro and basil, washed and chopped
$1/4$ cup cider vinegar
salt & pepper

YELLOW TOMATO COULIS: In a saucepan over medium-low heat, sweat onions in olive oil. Stir frequently and do not brown. When onions are translucent, add garlic and basil and cook for 2–3 minutes longer. Add tomatoes. Cook for 30 minutes or until tomatoes have stewed completely. Season with salt and pepper. Purée mixture in blender. Check for final seasoning and reserve at room temperature. Extra coulis may be refrigerated.

FRESH TOMATO SALSA: Mix all ingredients together in a mixing bowl and check for final seasoning.

GRILLED VEGETABLES: Preheat grill. Brush zucchini, squash and swordfish with olive oil and season with salt and pepper. When grill is hot, place squash slices on the grill. Rotate them at 90 degrees to get criss-cross grill marks. Turn them over after 2 minutes and remove to a cooler section of the grill.

SWORDFISH: Start swordfish steaks over hot part of the grill. Mark them with grill marks like vegetables. Once marked, move fish to area of grill with medium heat. It should take no more than 8–10 minutes for a steak that is $3/4$ inches thick

TO ASSEMBLE: Place about $1/4$ cup Yellow Tomato Coulis on each plate. Arrange 3 slices of squash around the center of the plate. Place swordfish steaks directly on top of squash and top with Fresh Tomato Salsa. Serve immediately.

Chef Ted Gidley, Clarke Cooke House, Newport, RI

189

Swordfish Maître d'Hôtel

SERVES 2

> 1 pound swordfish steaks (1-inch thick)
> melted butter
> Maître d'Hôtel Butter (see below)
> Lawry's® Seasoning Salt

Maître d'Hôtel Butter
> $1/2$ pound soft butter
> $1/2$ tablespoon chopped parsley
> 1 tablespoon lemon juice
> $1/2$ tablespoon chopped pimento
> $1/4$ teaspoon cayenne pepper

MAÎTRE D'HÔTEL BUTTER: Combine all ingredients for butter. Place on waxed paper and roll into a cylinder. Refrigerate until firm. May be stored in freezer.

SWORDFISH: Dip swordfish in melted butter and season lightly with Lawry seasoning. Preheat broiler. Place swordfish steaks in oven and broil 5-6 minutes per side. Just before sword is done, place two slices of Maître d'Hôtel Butter on top of swordfish. Serve immediately.

Grilled Swordfish with Basil Garlic Baste

SERVES 6–8

> 3 pounds swordfish (cut into $3/4$-inch thick steaks)

Basil Garlic Baste
> 1 cup salad oil
> 1 cup white wine vinegar or dry white wine
> 1 small clove garlic, mashed
> 1 tablespoon chopped parsley
> 1 teaspoon salt
> $1/2$ teaspoon dried basil
> $1/8$ teaspoon pepper

190

Preheat grill. Mix together all ingredients for Basil Garlic Baste. Marinate steaks in baste for 5-10 minutes. Remove fish from marinade. Grill approximately 10 minutes, turning once, and basting with marinade while cooking.

Swordfish Steak Oriental

SERVES 4

2 pounds swordfish steaks (1 inch thick)
1 tablespoon lemon juice
$1/4$ cup orange juice
1 clove garlic, chopped
$1/4$ cup soy sauce
$1/2$ teaspoon oregano
2 tablespoons ketchup
$1/2$ teaspoon pepper
2 tablespoons melted butter
2 tablespoons parsley, chopped

Cut steaks into individual portions. Place in single layer in shallow baking dish. Combine remaining ingredients; pour marinade over fish and refrigerate for 30 minutes. Preheat grill. Remove fish from marinade. Reserve marinade. Grill fish 6-8 minutes per side on preheated grill.

Reduce marinade in a small saucepan and pour over fish to serve.

Simply Elegant Grilled Swordfish

SERVES 6

6 swordfish steaks (1-inch thick)
salt & black pepper to taste
Maître d'Hôtel Butter (see page 190)

Marinade

2 cups oil
2 tablespoons soy sauce
2 tablespoons finely chopped shallots
1 cup dry white wine
dash of Tabasco

Season steaks with salt and pepper. Combine oil, soy sauce, shallots, white wine and Tabasco to make marinade. Marinate steaks for 1 hour in refrigerator, turning once.

Preheat and oil grill. Start steaks on hottest part of grill. When "marked" by grill bars, remove to the cooler part of the grill and finish cooking, approximately 10 minutes per inch of thickness, turning once.

Serve with Maître d'Hôtel Butter.

CAPE BLUEFISH

Cape bluefish are dark-meated fish harvested from the waters off Cape Cod. Cape blues have a delicious, rich flavor owing to their high level of beneficial omega 3 oils. A favorite catch of New England fishermen, blues are often served with acidic accompaniments such as tomatoes or lemon.

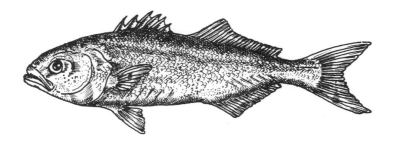

Foley's Cape Bluefish Dijonnaise

SERVES 6

3 pounds bluefish fillets
$1/4$ cup mayonnaise
1 tablespoon coarse-grained Dijon mustard
1 tablespoon lemon juice
1 tablespoon butter
1 tablespoon oil

Preheat grill. Divide bluefish fillets into 6 equal portions. Combine mayonnaise, mustard and lemon juice. Spread over bluefish portions. Heat sauté pan over medium-high heat. Add butter and oil. Sauté fillets for approximately 3 minutes per side. Remove from heat and finish cooking on grill, placing skin side down onto grill. Fish will be done in approximately 5 minutes. Serve hot.

193

Baked Cape Bluefish with Potatoes & Garlic

SERVES 6

2 bluefish fillets (about 1 pound each, skin on)
$1^1/_2$ pounds potatoes, peeled and thinly sliced
$2/_3$ cup extra virgin olive oil
$1^1/_2$ tablespoons chopped garlic
$1/_4$ cup chopped parsley
salt & freshly ground pepper

POTATOES: Preheat oven to 425°. Rinse potato slices in cold water and pat dry. Put potatoes in a large shallow baking dish. Add half of the olive oil, half the garlic, half the parsley, salt to taste and black pepper. Toss potatoes to coat; spread evenly over the bottom of the pan. Roast potatoes in oven for 12–15 minutes, until they are half done. Remove from oven.

BLUEFISH: Put fish fillets skin side down over partially roasted potatoes. Mix remaining olive oil, garlic and parsley in a small bowl and pour mixture over fish, distributing it evenly. Season again with salt and pepper and place in oven. After 10 minutes, baste fish with oil from the bottom of the dish. Return dish to oven and bake for 5–8 minutes more depending on thickness. Serve each portion with cooking liquid from pan.

STRIPED BASS

Each July we eagerly await the Nantucket striped bass season opening. This season remains open only until the quota is filled—usually the end of August. There are other bass in the sea but we think the Nantucket striped bass with its elegant, glistening, large flake and distinct sweet ocean flavor is the crème de la crème. Striped bass from other waters may be substituted when our prized Nantuckets are out of season!

Striped Bass with Shiitakes, Ginger & Tamari

SERVES 4

2 pounds striped bass fillets, cut into 4 portions
1 clove garlic, chopped
2 tablespoons sesame oil
1 tablespoon thinly sliced peeled ginger
$1/4$ cup tamari
$1/2$ cup clam juice
juice of $1/2$ lime
$1/2$ teaspoon tamarind
2 tablespoons rice wine vinegar
1 tablespoon maple syrup
4 ounces shiitake mushrooms, sliced
1 tablespoon scallions, chopped

Preheat oven to 450°. Sauté garlic in sesame oil over medium-low heat for 2–3 minutes. Stir in ginger and tamari. Add striped bass and sauté for 3 minutes per side. Remove fish and bake in oven for 6–8 minutes.

While fish is baking, add clam juice, lime juice, tamarind, rice wine vinegar and maple syrup to sauté pan. Simmer until flavors are well blended. Add shiitakes. Allow to simmer and reduce 7–9 minutes. Serve over striped bass. Garnish with scallions.

Eve Formisano, Providence, RI

195

Oven Poached Striped Bass with Tarragon Sauce

SERVES 6

6 striped bass fillets (6 ounces each)
2 tablespoons softened butter
3 shallots, finely chopped
juice of 1/2 lemon
salt & white pepper
1/2 cup dry white wine
1/2 cup dry vermouth
1 cup clam juice
1 cup heavy cream
3 tablespoons tarragon, chopped fine

Preheat oven to 325°. Butter the bottom of a 3-inch deep dish (ceramic, Pyrex or stainless steel) large enough to hold fish in one layer without crowding.

Sprinkle dish with shallots and add fish, skin down. Sprinkle fish with lemon juice and season lightly with salt and pepper. In a saucepan, bring wines and clam juice to a boil, then pour over the fish. Cover baking dish and place in the oven. Bake 6–10 minutes, depending on thickness of fish. With a spatula, carefully lift fish out and place on a warm platter. Cover and keep warm.

Strain juice back into saucepan. Boil to reduce to 1/2 cup. Add cream and reduce again, this time to a sauce consistency. Stir in tarragon; taste and adjust seasoning.

TO SERVE: Peel skin off fish, place on warm plates and spoon Tarragon Sauce over.

Grilled Striped Bass with Cilantro Pesto & Mango Salsa

SERVES 2

2 striped bass fillets (5 ounces each)
salt & pepper
6 tablespoons Cilantro Pesto (see below)
$1/2$ cup Mango Salsa (see below)

Cilantro Pesto

4 ounces cilantro
2 tablespoons pecans or pine nuts
1 medium-sized garlic clove, minced
6 tablespoons olive oil

Mango Salsa

$1/2$ red onion, sliced
1 red bell pepper, diced
2 mangos, diced
juice from $1/2$ orange
$1/2$ teaspoon minced parsley

CILANTRO PESTO: Add all ingredients to a blender and blend until smooth.

MANGO SALSA: Sauté red onion and bell pepper for 1–2 minutes. Add mango, orange juice and parsley. Sauté 2–3 minutes more.

STRIPED BASS: Salt and pepper bass fillets. Brush with olive oil. Grill on preheated grill for 8–10 minutes until fish flakes. Serve over Mango Salsa, topped with Cilantro Pesto.

Chef Bernard Pilon, Norwood Hills Country Club, St. Louis, MO

197

Grilled Striped Bass with Wilted Spinach & Warm Bacon/Mandarin Orange Vinaigrette

SERVES 4

Bacon/Mandarin Orange Vinaigrette
- $1/2$ pound bacon, diced
- 1 medium yellow onion, diced
- 1 tablespoon garlic
- 2 + 1 cans mandarin oranges (8 ounces each), drained
- 2 tablespoons brown sugar
- 2–4 tablespoons cider vinegar to taste
- salt & pepper to taste

Grilled Striped Bass
- 4 portions striped bass fillets (8 ounces each)
- olive oil
- salt & pepper to taste
- 1 pound fresh spinach, washed and de-stemmed

BACON/MANDARIN ORANGE VINAIGRETTE: Fry bacon over medium-high heat until fat is rendered. Reduce heat to medium-low and add onion. Cook for 2–3 minutes. Add garlic. Cook for 2–3 minutes. Add 2 cans of oranges and brown sugar; simmer for 15 minutes. Add 2 tablespoons of vinegar; simmer for 10 minutes. Season with salt and pepper; adjust vinegar to taste.

STRIPED BASS: Preheat grill. Lightly coat bass with olive oil and salt and pepper. Grill for approximately 6 minutes per side (assuming a $1^1/_2$-inch thick fillet).

TO SERVE: Toss $3/4$ of hot Bacon/Mandarin Orange Vinaigrette with fresh spinach to wilt. Mound on plate. Top with grilled striped bass and remaining vinaigrette. Garnish with remaining mandarin oranges.

MAHI MAHI

Mahi mahi is sometimes referred to as "dolphin fish" but it is not in any way related to dolphins! Caught in the Gulf of Mexico, mahi is a mild, firm fish. We like it best when grilled.

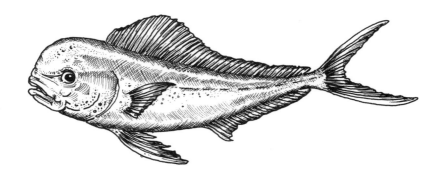

Mango Salsa-Topped Mahi Mahi

SERVES 4

1¹/₃ pounds mahi mahi
1 mango, pineapple or papaya, cut into
  bite-sized pieces
1 scallion, thinly sliced
1 lime, cut in half
ground black pepper
1 tablespoon olive oil

MANGO SALSA: In a small bowl, combine mango, green onion, juice from half of lime and pepper; stir.

MAHI MAHI: Preheat and oil grill. Drizzle mahi mahi with 1 tablespoon olive oil. Grill for 6–8 minutes per side depending on thickness. When fish is done, squeeze juice from remaining half of lime over fish. Serve fish with Mango Salsa on the side.

Mahi Mahi with Asparagus & Cashews

SERVES 4

4 mahi fillets (6 ounces each), cut into 1-inch chunks
1 tablespoon vegetable oil
$2/3$ cup vertically sliced yellow onion
$1^1/2$ tablespoons minced peeled fresh ginger
1 tablespoon fresh, grated orange rind
8 garlic cloves, minced
1 tablespoon grated lemon rind
1 tablespoon fresh lemon juice
1 teaspoon low-sodium soy sauce
1 teaspoon sherry or white wine vinegar
1 teaspoon honey
$1/2$ teaspoon dark sesame oil
$1/4$ teaspoon salt
4 cups sliced asparagus
$1/4$ cup coarsely chopped cashews
3 cups hot, cooked brown rice
cilantro for garnish

Combine soy sauce, vinegar, honey, sesame oil and salt; add asparagus and cashews; tossing well to coat. Heat vegetable oil in a large non-stick skillet over medium-high heat. Add onion; sauté 1 minute. Add ginger, orange rind and garlic; sauté 1 minute. Add fish; cook 3 minutes or until lightly browned stirring onion mixture in pan constantly to prevent burning. Sprinkle fish with lemon rind and juice. Add asparagus mixture to pan; cook 4 minutes or until fish flakes easily when tested with a fork. Sprinkle with cilantro and serve over rice.

Robert's Food Store, North Madison, CT

OCEAN PERCH

Ocean perch, a very different fish from lake perch, is harvested from the Gulf of Maine. It is typically sold with the skin on, so you may want to ask your fishmonger to skin it for you at the store. Ocean perch has a firm flesh and a very mild flavor.

Ocean Perch in a Pan

SERVES 4

8 ocean perch fillets, skinned
salt & pepper
3 tablespoons lemon juice
$1/2$ cup flour
2 tablespoons butter
2 tablespoons cooking oil
lemon wedges

Season fillets lightly with salt, pepper and lemon juice. Dredge lightly in flour. Coat sauté pan with no more than $1/8$ inch of a 50/50 mixture of melted butter and cooking oil; preheat. Sauté fillets over medium-high heat about 2 minutes on each side. Serve with lemon wedges on the side.

Deep Fried Ocean Perch

SERVES 4

8 ocean perch fillets, skinned
salt & pepper
3 tablespoons lemon juice
flour
1 egg
$1/2$ cup milk
1 cup Ritz crackers, rolled into fine crumbs

Season fillets lightly with salt, pepper and lemon juice. Dredge fillets lightly in flour. Dip floured fillets in beaten mixture of egg and milk. Dip in crumbs. Pat crumbs gently onto both sides of fillets. Fry fillets in preheated 375° oil until golden brown. For best results, place only one layer of fillets in fry basket at a time. Do not overcrowd.

Ocean Perch in a Pouch

SERVES 4

8 ocean perch fillets, skinned
1 green pepper, sliced
1 onion, sliced
salt & pepper
3 tablespoons lemon juice
1 tomato, sliced
2 teaspoons dried tarragon or basil
$1/2$ teaspoon dried oregano
2 tablespoons white wine or water
2 tablespoons melted butter (optional)

Preheat oven to 450°. Blanch green pepper and onion for 1 minute, drain. Lay fillet portions on individual squares of aluminum foil. Season lightly with salt, pepper and lemon juice. Layer peppers, onion and tomato on top. Season to taste with sprinkling of herbs. Moisten with melted butter and white wine. Fold aluminum foil around fish into tent-like shape, allowing space for steam to collect, and seal tightly. Bake or grill for 10 minutes or until fish flakes.

Serve in foil pouches so that each person can break the seal to smell the attractive aroma.

Sauces, Sides & Toppers

We offer the following sauces, sides and toppers to complement your seafood.

If you are short of time, crushed Ritz crackers or panko (Japanese breadcrumbs) are always winning toppers. Simply dip fillets in melted butter, then top with crumbs. Bake at 450° for 10 minutes per inch of thickness and your fish is finis!

For a zestier flavor, combine Dijon mustard with mayonnaise and spread atop the fish before adding crumbs — or simply spread and grill without any crumbs at all.

Start with great fish and you need little else!

Sauces, Sides & Toppers Recipes

Beurre Blanc

Use on any light fillet such as haddock, cod, flounder or hake.

1 shallot, diced
$1/2$ cup white wine
$1^1/_2$ sticks butter
chives, chopped

In saucepan, heat shallot and wine and let wine reduce. Whisk in butter slowly; do not brown.

Add chopped chives and serve over fish.

Carrot & Ginger Sauce

Great on haddock, halibut, cod.

2 medium/large carrots, sliced into disks
$1^1/_2$ tablespoons peeled and chopped ginger root
$1/2$ cup grape verius or orange juice
$1/4$ cup olive oil
2 tablespoons chopped cilantro
salt

Steam carrots and ginger in just enough water to cover. When cooked through and soft, add with liquid to blender. Blend with grape verius, olive oil, cilantro and salt to taste. Serve with any baked or grilled fish.

Zesty Breadcrumbs

Use with any fish!

2 cups fresh French bread with soft crust
1 tablespoon grainy mustard
1-2 tablespoons olive oil

Tear bread into 1-inch chunks. Place in food processor with mustard and enough olive oil to moisten. Process until bread is transformed into coarse crumbs. Use in any baked fish recipe in place of regular fresh breadcrumbs.

Spanish Sauce

Good for haddock, cod, pollock or monkfish.

$1/2$ green pepper, sliced
$1/2$ sweet red pepper, sliced
1 small stick celery, chopped
1 small onion, sliced
1 clove garlic, crushed
1 tablespoon butter
3 tomatoes, diced
1 tablespoon tomato purée
2 stuffed green olives, sliced
2 ounces diced mushrooms
2 ripe olives, coarsely chopped
chopped fresh parsley for garnish

Sauté peppers, celery, onion and garlic in butter. Add rest of ingredients and simmer for 5 minutes. Garnish with fresh chopped parsley. Serve over baked fish.

Remoulade Sauce

Serve aside fried fish or as a dipping sauce for crab.

1 cup mayonnaise
2 tablespoons mustard
$1/4$ cup capers, drained
2 tablespoons chopped fresh parsley
2 tablespoons chopped fresh chervil
2 tablespoons chopped fresh tarragon

Combine all and serve.

Sauce Aurora

Good for haddock, cod, pollock or monkfish.

1 tablespoon butter
$1/2$ tablespoon grated onion
2 tablespoons flour
1 cup milk
$1/2$ cup light cream
2 medium tomatoes, diced
1 tablespoon chopped fresh parsley
1 tablespoon sherry
salt & pepper

Melt butter, add onion and cook for 1 minute; do not brown. Add flour; stir until smooth. Add milk and cream; beat until smooth. Stir in diced tomatoes and parsley. Add sherry and simmer for 5 minutes. Season with salt and pepper.

Serve over baked or sautéed fish.

Niçoise Sauce

Good for haddock, cod, pollock or monkfish.

2 tablespoons butter
1 small onion, sliced
1 clove garlic, chopped
3 tomatoes, diced
1 tablespoon capers
1 tablespoon tomato purée
salt & pepper
anchovy fillets for garnish

Sauté onions in butter without browning. Stir in garlic, tomatoes, capers and tomato purée. Simmer for 20 minutes. Season with salt and pepper.

When serving, place an anchovy fillet on top if desired.

Scotty's Special Cocktail Sauce

For crabcakes, shrimp, crab and lobster.

1 cup ketchup
1 cup chili sauce
2 tablespoons finely chopped dill relish
1 tablespoon grated horseradish
1 dash Tabasco
1 dash Worcestershire sauce
$1/2$ teaspoon curry powder

Mix all together. It is better to keep in the refrigerator for at least a week before using. This lets the sauce blend and mellow.

Holiday Oyster Stuffing

1 pint shucked oysters
2 bunches green onions, chopped
1 small bunch of celery, chopped
1 bunch parsley, chopped fine
4 tablespoons butter
1 14-ounce package corn bread stuffing croutons
1 10-ounce can chicken broth
1 tablespoon Old Bay seasoning

Preheat oven to 375°. Sauté onion, celery and parsley in butter over medium-high heat for 3 minutes just until softened. Add oysters with liquid and sauté another 3 minutes until oysters curl. Pour croutons into a large mixing bowl and pour oyster mixture over croutons. Add broth and Old Bay seasoning and mix well. Place mixture in greased roasting pan. Bake for 20–25 minutes until golden brown and crispy.

Robert's Food Store, North Madison, CT

Foley's Passion Butter

1 pound butter
juice of $1/2$ lemon
2 dashes of Tabasco
2 tablespoons chopped garlic
1 4-ounce jar of chopped pimentos
2 tablespoons chopped fresh parsley
1 teaspoon kosher salt
1 teaspoon coarsely ground black pepper

Soften butter. Add the lemon juice and Tabasco. Knead in a large bowl. Add the remaining ingredients. Passion Butter can be divided into smaller quantities and frozen for future use.

We like Passion Butter on grilled fish — place it on top of fish steak right before it comes off the grill to allow it to begin to melt. It provides a stunning visual plate presentation.

Or — melt the Passion Butter and brush it on shrimp skewers or any other fish kabob.

Kid Fish

We've tested the following recipes on kids and they love them!

Be sure to check fillets for bones before serving to small children.

213

Kid Fish Recipes

Fish Nuggets

SERVES 4

1 pound fish fillet, cut into 2-inch strips
salt & pepper
2 teaspoons Dijon mustard
flour for dredging
1 egg
2 tablespoons milk
Ritz cracker crumbs
canola oil for frying

Cut fish pieces into uniform portion size. Season with salt and pepper. Paint lightly with Dijon mustard. Lightly dredge pieces in flour, then dip in egg wash made by beating egg with milk. Roll fillet pieces in Ritz cracker crumbs and pat crumbs gently onto both sides of fillets. Fry in fresh oil at 375° for approx. 2–3 minutes or until golden brown. Drain on paper towels.

Tex-Mex Whitefish

SERVES 4

$1^{1}/_{2}$ pounds mild, boneless fish fillets
 (hake, haddock, cod)
$^{1}/_{2}$ cup prepared salsa – mild
1 cup Monterey jack cheese

Preheat oven to 450°. Place fish in single layer in shallow baking dish or casserole. Fold thinner tail portions under to ensure even doneness. Spoon salsa over fillets. Top with grated cheese. Bake for 12 minutes per inch of thickness of fillets.

215

Mama Mia, It's Italian!

SERVES 4

$1^1/_2$ pounds mild, boneless fish fillets
(hake, haddock, cod)
1 cup prepared marinara sauce
$^1/_4$ cup grated Parmesan cheese
$^1/_4$ cup mozzarella cheese, grated

Preheat oven to 450°. Place fish in single layer in shallow baking dish or casserole. Fold thinner tail portion under to ensure even doneness. Spoon sauce over fillets. Top with grated cheese. Bake for 12 minutes per inch of thickness of fillets.

Hake Cheesewiches

Haddock, cod, or pollock can be substituted for hake.

SERVES 4

4 boneless hake portions (6 ounces each)
$^1/_2$ cup melted butter
1 cup crushed Ritz cracker crumbs
4 slices American cheese
4 sandwich rolls

Preheat oven to 450°. Slice fillets into 2-inch long and $^3/_4$-inch wide strips. Dip strips in melted butter and roll in Ritz cracker crumbs. Place strips in groups of 3 on a cookie sheet with 1 tablespoon of water. Bake for 5–7 minutes, until fish flakes and crumbs are golden. Place a slice of cheese over each group of 3 and bake until cheese melts.

Serve on toasted sandwich rolls with ketchup or tartar sauce.

Fish on a Stick

Alexsandria Gillespie, a daughter of Foley account manager Rance Gillespie, is responsible for the origin of this recipe. She would only eat fish if it was on a stick, so Dad developed this just for her. It's a winner with all ages—we call it Sole Satay and pair it with Chipotle dipping sauce when serving it to the over-18 crowd!

SERVES 6

$1^1/_2$ **pounds flounder fillets**
salt & pepper
$1/_2$ **cup flour**
$1/_2$ **cup Italian breadcrumbs**
1 cup corn flakes, pounded
1 egg, slightly beaten
$3/_4$ **cup milk**
canola oil for frying
wooden skewers

Season flounder with salt and pepper. Combine flour, breadcrumbs and corn flakes. Combine egg and milk. Cut each fillet into 4 equal pieces.

Thread flounder pieces onto wooden skewers from top to bottom by weaving stick in and out of fish. Dip "fish sticks" into egg wash then dredge in flour-crumb-corn flake mixture.

Pour oil into 2 quart pan until it is $1/_4$ inch deep. Heat oil to approximately 375° (check with thermometer). Deep fry until golden, approximately 2–3 minutes.

Serve with your child's favorite dipping sauces.

217

Index

220